MEMORIES OF
WAPPING
1900–1960

To my Father and Uncle Bernie

My Father (right) and Uncle Bernie, Poplar, 1919.

'COULDN'T AFFORD THE EELS'

MEMORIES OF WAPPING
1900–1960

MARTHA LEIGH

Front cover: The Pool of London 1949. Boys from Wapping watch from an old wooden dock as a tug boat steams past on the Thames. (Copyright Getty Images)

Back cover: Jubilee of inauguration of St George's Mission 8 July 1906.

First published 2008
Reprinted 2008, 2010, 2011

The History Press
The Mill, Brimscombe Port
Stroud, Gloucestershire, GL5 2QG
www.thehistorypress.co.uk

© Martha Leigh 2011

The right of Martha Leigh to be identified as the Author
of this work has been asserted in accordance with the
Copyrights, Designs and Patents Act 1988.

British Library Cataloguing in Publication Data.
A catalogue record for this book is available from the British Library.

ISBN 978 0 7524 4709 4

Typesetting and origination by
The History Press.
Printed and bound in Great Britain by
Marston Book Services Limited, Didcot

CONTENTS

Acknowledgements

I wish to thank the following for their help:

For getting me started; John Eversley, Sally Hull, Pat Hoddinott, the East London Supported Research Programme (ELENoR) and the London Deanery for granting me a sabbatical.

Thanks to Gerry Bennett, Professor of Healthcare of the Elderly at Barts and the London Queen Mary's School of Medicine and Dentistry, who was my supervisor until his tragic death in April 2003. His humanity as a mentor and a doctor was inspiring. I am also grateful to Mira Vogel at Queen Mary, who used some of the material in this book for medical student training, for her enthusiasm and encouragement.

For help in recruiting interviewees I am very grateful to Richard Mitchell, Adam Stern, Paul Nottingham, Jonathan Graffy, Jasmine Ali, Eileen Callagher, Maxine Kohl, Eileen Griffiths and Sheila Wood.

For invaluable help with computing, I give special thanks to my brother, John Leigh.

I am also grateful to Thaya Parathayalasekaran for the time he spent scanning pictures for me.

I thank Maurice Foley for background information on docking history and Sylvia Coote for allowing me to see the unpublished manuscript by Ellen Kemp.

For reading parts of the manuscript critically, I thank John Leigh, John Eversley, Bronwen Saunders, Paul Nixon, Peter Bavington, Robert Thorne and most especially Linda Proud-Smith.

Thanks too to John Eversley for pointing me to useful sources of information.

For their support and encouragement, my warm thanks to Geraldine Cooke, Anthony Rudolf and William Fishman.

I am very grateful to Father Jones for allowing me to use the St Peter's Church archive and his generosity in lending me such wonderful photographs. Thanks also to Father Samuels for allowing me to use the St Patrick's Church archive.

My thanks to Bob Aspinall for allowing me to browse and use the PLA archive at the Museum in Docklands.

Thanks to Christopher Lloyd and Malcolm Barr-Hamilton at Tower Hamlets Local History Library for their kindness and helpfulness on my many visits to the library and for enabling me to use the library's photographs.

Thanks to Dennis (Sonny) Peters for the loan of his photograph collection, Rosemary Taylor, Michael Billig, Patrick Connolly and John Joslin for help with researching photographs.

Thanks to Edward Graves and many other inhabitants of Wapping who clarified issues and provided extra information and also to all the people in Wapping who generously lent their family photographs for reproduction.

Finally, I shall never be able to thank my husband Huw Saunders enough, for his continuous loving interest, involvement and patience throughout the book's long journey to publication.

INTRODUCTION

For nearly two centuries, the Port of London was the busiest in the world. Through it flowed all the riches of the British Empire, and right at its heart was the small community of Wapping. Situated on the north bank of the Thames, the London Docks at Wapping made a vital contribution to the nation's trading prosperity until they were closed in the late sixties.

By 1987, when I first came to work there as a GP, the inland waterway system of docks had been filled in and landscaped, derelict areas were being turned into pricey new housing developments and old warehouses into luxury riverside apartments. With the redevelopment and change in population came a complete transformation of the character of what had been a rather secret enclave.

In the course of my work I have visited many older people in their homes, people who had lived in Wapping all their lives, and in many cases, whose family had been there for generations. This privileged insight awakened an urge to find out more about life in Wapping in the early part of the twentieth century. Here was an opportunity to preserve people's memories of a bygone world, and I realised that I would have to get on with this work before it was too late. I already knew many people who had died, taking their stories with them. In 2002-2003 I took a sabbatical, which was funded by the NHS, in order to conduct interviews with older people who had grown up in Wapping between the two World Wars. The study was passed by the local ethics committee which was necessary because some of the interviewees were also my patients. The consent, insurance, and disclaimer paperwork required by the ethics committee unfortunately probably deterred some people from agreeing to an interview. I interviewed thirty-one people who were mostly in their seventies and eighties. Four of them were in their nineties. There were twenty women and eleven men and most, but not all, of the interviewees were from docking families. Three were professional people who came to work in Wapping, and a few of them grew up just outside. I have included some of their testimony where it was relevant. For the purpose of confidentiality, the names of the interviewees have been changed and any other contributors have only been named with their explicit consent. I have stated the date of birth of each speaker in order to give the reader a sense of historical context.

I recorded and transcribed each interview word for word. Whilst relishing the lively cockney vernacular, I often found this quite a challenge. The material covered a broad spectrum of themes out of which I have formed separate chapters. Although inevitably, by ordering and classifying the material from conversations into themes I have imposed my own selection process, I have tried to represent the range of views presented to me accurately, indicating which ones were typical, whilst not overlooking those of people whose opinions were peculiar to themselves. As the interviewer, I allowed people to talk about what interested them most. I found, for example, that they had far more to say about their childhood than the impact on them of the introduction of the NHS.

Oral history offers memories which are necessarily subjective and selective. I was brought up with stories about the East End from my father and uncle (born in 1915 and 1913 respectively) who grew up in a slum in Poplar. Their father was a Jewish tailor who had come from Lithuania in 1908. He remembered that throughout his childhood, his father used to say 'When I was your age (whatever that happened to be!) I was crossing Europe on foot'. My father's mother died when she was only thirty-five, leaving her sons, aged nine and eleven, to the care of their hapless father who drowned his sorrows with alcohol. During their childhood they, like many poor East End children, were periodically farmed out to relatives whenever their father could not cope, and it was only on joining the army that they were able to count on having a square meal. Happily, I grew up in material comfort, but I was all the more struck by the contrast between my life and theirs. I wanted to find out more.

And so it was no accident that I went to work as a GP in Wapping, approximately two miles from my father's old house in Poplar, and have continued to work there ever since.

What follows is not a comprehensive overview as one might find in a reference book or museum, but rather more of a patchwork – a more focused and personal view of people's everyday lives expressed in their own words. The words bring them to life with an immediacy just as compelling as the photographs, capturing the unique flavour of their experience and the personality of the speaker. I have reproduced people's words as faithfully as possible, resorting to editing (in square brackets) only where absolutely necessary for the sake of clarity. Historical facts are well known. The feelings of ordinary people are not, and unless their voices are preserved, future generations will only be able to guess at them.

To the eyes of many old Wappingites the redevelopment in the eighties was not welcome. Ernie, living alone in a council flat in Wapping in his nineties, complained of feeling 'a prisoner in these four walls'. His flat, equipped with all modern comforts, was kept immaculately clean by his daughters. Pointing from his window with a shaky hand, he showed me where the long-since demolished slum of his childhood had once stood. He was transported back into the tiny house once again, crammed in with his large family, with the wonderful smell of his mother's cooking and the noisy street outside with chickens running all over the place. In his mind's eye he could still see ships passing by in the dock just beyond. I hope that this book will offer an insight into some aspects of the culture, history and everyday lives of the community that once existed in Wapping and that the reader will gain a richer sense of life in those times.

1

WAPPING AND ITS PEOPLE

In 1969 the London Docks at Wapping closed down, marking the end of an era.[1] The character of Wapping and its people had been shaped by the river for generations, and this event brought a traditional way of life to an end. The people in this book speak of life in the first half of the twentieth century, a time when this community revolved around the docks.

In many ways, the character of its inhabitants bore similarities with other East Enders and working-class Londoners. Yet Wapping always had its own distinct identity because it was virtually an island. Bordered by the Thames to the south and the Ratcliffe Highway to the north, its only links to the outside world before the docks were closed were its four bridges: the Hermitage bridge at the Pierhead, the two bascule bridges at New Gravel Lane[2] and at Glamis Road and the one at Old Gravel Lane, the first iron-swing bridge in the world.

Beyond Wapping was a much more cosmopolitan area. Within a mile there were the Chinese in Limehouse, the Jews in Whitechapel and the Italians, Maltese and Caribbean people of Cable Street. These streets were teeming with sailors and people of all nationalities. Grace lived five minutes' walk away from Wapping, off the Ratcliffe Highway:

> Ah, yes, they used to come through, and they were all big blond giants and I suppose we used to flirt with them in our own way ... I used to scrub that stone and then you'd get the whitening and you'd whiten it along ... and the Dutch, they used to come through, clonking along in their clogs – painted clogs.
>
> Grace (born 1921)

The system of inland waterways leading into the docks cut Wapping off from all this, since it was only possible to set foot there by crossing one of the bridges.[3] Wapping was insular, both in the literal geographical sense and in the mentality of its people:

> Course you had all the bridges round us which was like an island – all we knew was one another.
>
> Elsie (born 1913)

Even people who lived at the other end of Old Gravel Lane beyond the bridge could not claim to be 'Wappingites' because they were from 'over the bridge'. It was exceptional for outsiders to cross over the bridges into Wapping unless they worked there or needed to come to the hospital. This was an unwritten rule:

> If you didn't live in Wapping you couldn't come over that bridge.
>
> Kathleen (born 1934)

People were regularly kept waiting for the bridges to go up to let cargo ships in and out of the docks. The sound of a bell or siren warned people several times a day that the bridge was about to go up and the traffic would have to stop. This was very irritating for those who were in a hurry to get to work or school, and some people would then run to the nearest bridge to avoid being delayed. George's son said that when he was a child, the lightermen, who all knew him, used to lift him down and pass him across from one barge to another, but for most people 'catching a bridger' was part of life.

The Pool of London, 1949. A man is working on a jetty with two tug boats in the foreground and Tower Bridge in the distance. (Copyright Getty Images)

Shadwell Bridge. The bascule bridge was raised using hydraulic power from the Wapping pumping station in order to let ships into Shadwell Docks.

All had the hump when they got there, cursing the bridge mechanic who swung the bridge.

Victor (born 1930)

Grace, who went to school in The Highway, outside Wapping, remembers the Wapping girls in her class.

Girls used to come running in all out of breath and they said 'Sorry, Miss, we got a bridger!' – they'd run all the way!

Grace (born 1921)

The river and the docks were the background scenery of the lives of all the inhabitants of the island. From their windows, people could see the masts of ships, the tops of cranes and the smoke from the funnels of tugs bringing the ships into the docks via Shadwell basin. They could hear the mournful sound of ships' hooters both night and day as they entered and left the dock. The river was always busy:

You had boats and tugs and barges … it was actually crammed tight with craft going up and craft coming down. Now, you could fall asleep in a rowing boat!

Ted (born 1926)

Lightermen were a familiar sight on the river as they manoeuvred their barges with a long pole to prevent them from colliding with other craft. In winter the river was often covered in thick fog.

During the first half of the twentieth century, London was the biggest port in the world, handling at least one-third of all Britain's seaborne trade. The whole waterfront from St Katherine's Dock downstream to the Prospect of Whitby public house was lined with warehouses stuffed with goods from all over the globe. Food and drink made up a significant proportion of the cargoes: there were the huge Ceylon tea warehouses at Colonial, Oliver's and Orient Wharves, while cocoa and coffee were stored at New Crane Wharf, sugar at St Bride's and lime juice and spirits were bottled at the British and Foreign Wharf. Boats came in loaded with bananas, oranges, tomatoes, nuts, grain, sugar or spices. The Guinness boats came

Shipping in the western basin of the London Dock, 1955. (Copyright Museum of London/PLA collection)

Wine quays and warehouses at the London Docks, 1920. (Copyright Museum of London/PLA collection)

across from Dublin carrying general cargo such as dairy produce as well as stout. Materials such as cork from Portugal, rubber from Malaya, elephant tusks, Belgian tiles, Roman stone and marble all came to the London Docks. Vaults several miles long situated underneath the London Docks stored most of the wines and sherry imported into the country each year, as well as whisky, brandy and rum.

Built originally for the very purpose of protecting merchandise from theft in 1800, the docks were closed to the public. The high dock walls designed by the architect of Dartmoor Prison, Daniel Asher Alexander (1768-1846) were guarded by a policeman at every gate. They obliterated the view of the river except in a few places. Audrey remembered the excitement she had felt as a child on being granted a privileged glimpse of life behind the dock walls, when she was invited on board a steam ship from Hamburg because her uncle knew the captain.

Many local businesses depended on the river and the docks; the tin factory, the sack and tarpaulin factories, the rope factory, the rag and waste-paper company and various haulage and marine salvage firms to name but a few. Smoke billowed into the sky from the black, white-and-red-striped funnels of Alexander's tugs as they towed the big ships into the docks. The first thing many people noticed on emerging from the underground station onto Wapping High Street was the heavenly smell of spices wafting from the open shutters of the spice factory:[4]

> You could see the big cog, the big wheels. They used to shake the different spices in, and these wheels used to be turning and grinding and the fumes was just marvellous.
>
> Ted (born 1926)

The fragrance of cinnamon and nutmeg mingled with that of freshly milled pepper. You could not walk past the spice factory without sneezing when the windows were open. The air was sometimes heavy with the perfume of soaps from Gibbs' factory, the smell of the thick, dark brown foot sugar from St John's Wharf and hops from the brewery. There was also the delicious scent of oranges mixed with onions coming from Morocco Wharf. Less pleasant was the sour odour of soot from all the coal fires burning in every home, and even worse, the musty stench that rose from the river. The many factories just outside Wapping caused a lot of pollution:

> Up the road was a biscuit factory – I forget their name[5] – and all the factories on the Highway and further up and at Commercial Street used to be BDV[6] and behind it was Truman's brewery – oh, Mann and Crossman's was up the road as well. You think of all that and all the docks and all the tugs and everything coming out with all the smoke.
>
> Janet (born 1921)

> You could smell Batger's sweet shop, you could smell Meredith and Drew's biscuit shop, you could smell the spices from the docks that were all banged up in these warehouses and all those smells, they mingled! And it was the most wonderful smell on earth! You can almost smell it now!
>
> Grace (born 1921)

Some of the vast warehouses such as Metropolitan Wharf on Wapping Wall had overhead wooden footbridges spanning the High Street. These 'walk-acrosses' were used to transfer goods above ground. Mary's son had a happy memory of being transported as a young child by a docker from one side of the overhead bridge to the other in a tea chest. Grand public buildings such as the Port of London Authority Building at the Hermitage, the Pumping Station and the impressive Georgian houses built for the dockmasters at the Pierhead overlooking the river, stood cheek by jowl with shabby tenement blocks and tiny cramped houses in narrow, pokey backstreets and unlit alleyways.

The importance of the river and the sea was reflected in the names of some pubs such as the China Ship and the Jolly Sailor – and of course the famous Prospect of Whitby.[7] Until the Second World War there was a pub on practically every street corner.[8] This perhaps compensated for the lack of living space in people's homes. There were also many dockers' cafés. The Gas Works, which closed after an explosion in 1935, was an important source of local employment. Gibbs' soap factory off Wapping High Street, its chimney a familiar landmark, was another.[9]

King George V and Queen Mary opening King Edward VII Park, 1922. This park, just east of Wapping, was also known as 'Shadwell Park'. In the background is a stone shaft with an inscription in memory of King Edward VII. Also in the park is a memorial with the names of the many famous navigators who set sail from Wapping in the sixteenth century. (Copyright Tower Hamlets Local History Library)

There were several other important public buildings: St George's in the East Hospital,[10] the Board of Guardians offices, and the three churches, St Peter's and St John of Wapping (both Anglican) and St Patrick's (Catholic). Each church had its own school.[11] There were two other schools which were not affiliated to a church: the Hermitage School and Brewhouse Lane School. In addition to the churches, there was Benn's Chapel and Meeting House.

The dangers of the river were known to everyone and most people could relate stories of drowning or near escapes. The river was even more hazardous during heavy fogs, known as 'pea-soupers' which could reduce the visibility to scarcely 1ft ahead and bring the river traffic to a standstill. The stretch of water at Wapping was known to be particularly treacherous. Lucy could recall watching divers putting on their helmets to explore the murky depths, presumably for dead bodies, when she was a child. At that time the river police[12] had their own mortuary. Grace and her friends were morbidly fascinated with the suicides by drowning that occurred during the Great Depression:

> The river police [with their] river launches, they used to come along and then – the kids were terrible callous, they said 'Another dead body coming up!' and we'd all run and try and see the dead body.
>
> Grace (born 1921)

People could get access to the river from one of the six old 'stairs':

> There was some steps and there was the river, the muddy old river, and the boys – a lot of them must have got killed in the war – and they used to come down with an old towel and an old pair of trunks and swim in the water. Well that river Thames had terrible undercurrents and I've actually seen a boy almost drowning with his arms held up (like that) ... and a docker, he just got up – and this man jumped in, jumped in and saved him.
>
> Grace (born 1921)

Not only was there the danger of being swept away by the tide but there were also the hazards of the heavy pollution of the water at that time. During the first two-thirds of the twentieth century the river became progressively more toxic until eventually, by the 1950s, there ceased to be any fish in it whatsoever. The level of pollution could be seen from the red colour of the mud at low tide caused by a sludge worm which thrived in contaminated waters:[13]

> Boy Fuller, he got sucked under a barge and got drownded and Andrews, he contracted a germ from out of there and he died, cos at that time the Thames wasn't like it [is now] – like you had dogs, cats and rats and lumps of wood and everything and you'd be swimming about, just pushing them out of the way.
>
> Ted (born 1926)

Until the Second World War there were two communities in Wapping: the Protestants and the Catholics. People belonging to neither the Protestant nor the Irish Catholic community were conspicuous, and foreigners such as the German who ran the post office stood out in people's memories. While Protestants had been living in the area for many centuries, Irish Catholics had started to settle in Wapping in the mid-eighteenth century and later worked as navvies in the building of the London Docks which started at the turn of the nineteenth century. Further immigration continued in waves during the potato famines between 1846 and 1851. Many Catholics born in the 1920s remembered their older relatives talking about 'the Old Country' in Irish accents and Irish traditions were still alive in many families:

> Well, my Gran was a wonderful woman ... she used to know all the rebel songs, she used to teach me, you know what I mean.
>
> Jack (born 1924)

Audrey, a Protestant woman in her seventies, described the relationship between the Protestants and the Catholics when she was growing up:

> The poorest were the Irish, of course. There was quite a lot of animosity [between the Catholics and the Protestants] but not on a personal level. I mean, we knew quite a lot of families in those days that we were friendly with. But they were very Irish in those days because they'd only fairly recently arrived.
>
> Audrey (born 1927)

Inevitably, where the community was so enclosed and the size of families very large – sixteen children in a family was not unheard of – there was a lot of intermarriage. Everybody knew everybody else, so much so that to many people it felt as if the whole community was an extended family:

> Cos Mr Gallagher, he was an O'Brien, like, they were all interlinked, like Mr Gallagher's wife was an O'Brien, can't you see? ... and over the Hermitage, the O'Briens and the O'Callaghans, good gracious, you had sixteen of one and ten of the other and that's twenty six before you start!
>
> Ted (born 1926)

Children could address any adult as 'uncle' or 'aunty'. Married women were usually known by their maiden name and children were referred to as 'so and so's boy or girl' using their mother's maiden name rather than their father's surname.

> They don't care who your father is, your father's nothing! Nothing your old man! It was always the women.
>
> Jack (born 1924)

It was a clannish, or even tribal type of community. Many people regarded it as a village. When Elsie was an old lady and had moved a little way out of Wapping, she continued to regard it as home:

> I mean, if I feel a bit blue at anytime, I just get on a bus and go down Wapping and have a trot round and I'll find it very easy to find someone to talk to.
>
> Elsie (born 1913)

Practically everybody stressed the friendliness and helpfulness of their neighbours. Lizzie (although conceding she might be biased!) even referred to the people of Wapping as a 'special breed' in this respect. Most people described how they were in constant contact with their neighbours, enjoying a relationship of complete trust, sharing both good times and bad. People talked nostalgically about the custom of leaving the front door key on a string which could be reached through the letter box by a neighbour whenever they wanted to let themselves in. Some people just left their doors unlocked without fear of being burgled:

> The old Wapping people were marvellous people. You'd go to bed and leave your street door open all night – you didn't have to bar yourself in like you do now.
>
> Mary (born 1912)

> And in them days when me mother went out ... there used to be a wall ... and Mother used to leave the insurance there – the money – or the milk money – no fear of anyone coming up and stealing that. Just left it there, that's how honest people were in them days.
>
> Tom (born 1923)

Jack made a joke of this.

> I mean years ago, when I was a boy, you left your door open all night because you had nothing to nick but kids ... if anyone come to rob, you'd shout out, 'You find anything down there, you let us know and we'll share it!'
>
> Jack (born 1924)

The kettle was always on the stove ready to make tea for neighbours and relatives who were constantly popping in and out of each others' houses. Women in their pinafores took a break from the housework to chat on their steps:

> And if your Mum was in hospital the next door neighbour looked after you. Know what I mean, that's how it was.
>
> Jack (born 1924)

Neighbours appeared on the scene to offer advice whenever there was a crisis, such as a sudden illness or death. Their opinion carried a lot of weight. Mary recalled the scene when her mother was suddenly taken ill:

Two of the neighbours that lived over here came up to see her and I says to them: 'Do you know, I think my Mum's had a stroke' and Mrs Brown, she was, and Mrs Green, they were very, very nice people, so she said 'Yes, I think she has by the sound of it.'

Mary (born 1912)

When food was short people helped each other out:

There used to be an old Mrs Healy who lived next door to me Nan … Me Nan was well stocked up. If she went out, her key was always in the door on a lump of string … If she had nothing, or if she'd sort of run out of something for the kids, she'd get that string out, go in my Nan's and help herself. When she got paid at the end of the week, she'd buy that and give it back to my Nan. You know, she always used to say, like 'I've been in and took this' or 'been in and took that' – they could do it, and they never robbed from one another.'

But as I was saying, you could get pot herbs and all that. They used to make stews, people did, and if there was a bit left over, they'd say 'take that to the old feller next door'.

They also shared any windfalls:

They always used to say it 'dropped off the back of a lorry'. There was tea, booze, everything – there was always something going, everybody helped one another.

Kathleen (born 1934)

Dockers helped to keep people going when they were short of essentials:

[If] they see that old girl going along, they'd run down and give 'em a bag of tea, a little [bag] of sugar.

Kathleen (born 1934)

It's the sort of thing you can talk about it now, people down here, I reckon, actually lived off the docks.

Bob (born 1933)

Not everyone in Wapping was poor, however. There were some businessmen and their families, city workers, print workers, shopkeepers and publicans, and a few wealthy people who stood out because they owned a car before the Second World War. There was what Lizzie described as 'the elite of Wapping'. In 1912, the mayor of Stepney lived in Wapping.[14] He owned a telephone and had a chauffeur-driven car, luxuries which must have seemed astonishing to ordinary people at that time. The clergy, both Catholic and Protestant, were a very influential presence and the community of nuns in a grand building at Wapping Pierhead was established at least 100 years ago.[15] In those days you could easily tell a person's class from the way they were dressed. Mary's grandfather was a snob who had wanted Mary's mother to marry somebody with 'spats and canary coloured gloves' instead of her father, who came from a lower rung of the social ladder. Jack Banfield mentions how the ordinary people of Wapping looked up to the local vet who made a splash when driving round Wapping in his pony van in the twenties, wearing polished riding boots.[16] The men in suits who worked in the municipal offices stood out amongst the ordinary people. Publicans and landladies dressed up to impress – the publican might sport an Albert (a gold watch on a chain), the landlady her finest clothes and jewellery – 'the more diamonds the better'. People of all classes demonstrated a sense of self-respect through their clothing. Norman, who came from a poor family, owned a beautiful photograph of his mother dressed in furs. Ada's mother would never leave the house without her hat and gloves.

Living in a close-knit community led people to feel a sense of responsibility towards each other:

I mean, I tell you what, it was such a clean place, you know, you lived in a flat and the stairs, like you all had to take your turn cleaning the stairs, no-one wet or done wees or that, and if you had a neighbour that didn't take their turn you wouldn't row with them but you'd tell 'em it was their turn.

Lizzie (born 1927)

People were very concerned about how their neighbours would judge them. After her mother died, Lizzie and her sister used to clean her father's bedsit. He said to her, 'You ain't wetting my floors – you'll give me rheumatism!', but she and her sister used to say:

Norman's mother in furs.

Look, we've come up to clean, if you're took bad and a neighbour comes in you won't get talked about, we will, leaving you like this!'

Lizzie (born 1927)

There was little privacy. If there was any disturbance in the neighbourhood, large numbers of people came out to watch and 'put their oar in'. If it came to a showdown the protagonists ran the risk of being shamed in public. Saturday nights were usually noisy after the pubs closed with drunken arguments and fights. From the insiders' point of view however, Wapping was a vibrant and mostly harmonious place, with a lot of shouting and bawling perhaps, but no serious injury:

No sooner they've had a good fight, they'd shake hands and go and get drunk. They never held it against one another. And then, more likely after that, they'd go round to one another's houses and have a party. Like with my Dad on Saturday night, my Dad used to play in the jazz band, and his mate used to play accordion, our uncle used to play banjo and there was another man, relation to one of the other girls, used to play the accordion and they used to fetch the piano out in the street when the pubs shut and it'd end up we're all out in the street having a party. And that was really lovely.

Kathleen (born 1934)

Weapons were not generally used during fights and several people seemed to regard fist fighting as a type of good-natured sport:

But one of my brother-in-laws and his brother, they used to have terrible fights and it was a pleasure to watch 'em – you would see a good fight. And they enjoyed it.

Ernie (born 1913)

Women often joined in. Mary gave the following account of a fracas:

She was a lovely woman, came from a really high class family, but the man she married was a toe-rag and one or two of her brothers started on him one day and the biggest one hit him, so course I went down and I went in, didn't I, so someone went and told, where I hit him, that he was on the floor. I see he'd come out after me, there was all the women standing either side of the court, my Mum was there … I was a terror, believe me – and she went in and I don't know if you remember them brass fire tongs – she went in and got them out to hit me with.

Mary (born 1912)

People were quick to use their fists to defend their family or their honour:

I will not stand for liberty takers. Taking the mick out of someone, a quip – I've gotta get up.

Jack (born 1924)

A handcart, kept in a wooden hut, was used by the police to transport a man to the local police station just outside Wapping when necessary. If he was drunk and disorderly, or causing a disturbance for any other reason they could strap him down. Children loved all the commotion:

They used to frogmarch 'em up Prusom Street to King David Lane when they were drunk coming out of the pub [The Cuckoo]. None of them were my family. All us kids used to follow them and run after them and then sometimes they used to get a stretcher … when they'd had a fight.

Elsie (born 1913)

Public events drew large crowds. At funerals, for instance, the churches would be filled to overflowing with friends, neighbours and relatives. Children also gathered together to see the street entertainers such as the 'nancy men' – drag artistes:

Sundays we used to have a man come round with his organ (portable)[17] and his wife, and all us children used to sit on the kerb, and he used to be in the middle of the road, and he had a funny eye and he got the nickname of 'mutton eye' – everybody knew him and his wife used to sing, and all in Jubilee Buildings used to kneel on the window ledges and put the window down.

Lizzie (born 1927)

Some personalities stood out in people's memories. Everybody remembered Mog Murphy, the eccentric owner of the Turk's Head pub who swore like a trooper at her customers. Ted told a story about another well known character, a man as tall as a giant:

But there was one person in there, Charmaine. He was as big as me ... he went into Morocco Wharf, picked up a case of oranges, marched out with it on his shoulder, took 'em in St George's up to the children's ward and tipped them on the floor in there and walked out again!

Ted (born 1926)

Policemen wheeling a culprit on a three-wheeled stretcher. The offender had probably been drunk and disorderly. A crowd of children is looking on.

Wapping Park was another centre of community life. People who grew up in the twenties and thirties remembered the park attendant with affection because she used to give them a plant every spring. In summer she wore a straw boater and a starched apron. Ernie had fond memories of his seven sisters dressing up to go to dances held in the park:

> And in the park there, on a Thursday night, they used to have a military band playing in the bandstand and my sisters used to be done up in their big hats. They used to think they were lovely! Well, they *were* lovely!
>
> Ernie (born 1913)

This warmth and community spirit was strictly contained within Wapping.

Bob, who came from Cable Street, all of a quarter of a mile away, said that when he was courting Kathleen, a Wapping girl, in about 1950, he had had to be escorted into Wapping by a bodyguard, for fear of being attacked by locals. At that time cab drivers would not come into Wapping and even policemen went about in pairs. The only time Wapping was 'open' to the outside world was for the great annual church festivals at Corpus Christi and Petertide.

If Wapping appeared forbidding to the rest of the world, to the people of Wapping themselves it felt like a haven. Mistrust of the unknown was part of a territorial attitude. Cable Street was full of foreigners and most people who did not live there in the twenties and thirties were afraid to go there. Then, during the Second World War, it became a red-light district and a pocket of extreme poverty where crime, knifings and prostitution were rife. Some girls like Janet, were forbidden to set foot outside Wapping by their parents:

> I was to keep away from Pennington Street – it was like 'Incubator Alley'. There used to be the dock wall down one side and all houses – aw – incubator alley. And Juniper Street up Stepney, that was another incubator alley.
>
> Janet (born 1921)

Occasionally lascars came ashore in Wapping.[18] Ada's mother refused to send her children to school in case they bumped into them as they came off the ships. She was taken to task for this by a school official. In the end the whole family moved nearer to the school so that the children were less likely to meet them.

Outsiders could be just as prejudiced about Wapping. Because it had such a bad reputation, people were advised not to mention it when applying for work. Doris recalled that when she left school before the Second World War, she had lied and said she was from the Parish of St George in the East at her first job interview.

People in their eighties and nineties could bring to mind in vivid detail the large number of shops along Old Gravel Lane, one of Wapping's main streets. At over ninety years of age, Ada could list twenty shops, describe their exact location and name and discuss all the shopkeepers who were there in the twenties when she was young. She firmly believed that there was more choice and variety in those days. In a small community like Wapping, people had personal relationships with their shopkeepers and referred to the shop by the name of its owner. They delighted in the shopkeepers' eccentricities: the man in the post office always used to wear straw hats, and there was a 'wizened' café owner called 'Bang Bang' who stood out probably because he was black.[19] Nellie and Lizzie took pleasure in recalling the favourite sweetshop of their childhood:

> You used to go in there and he used to have a machine with a thing across that chopped the toffee up. And we used to go there and get the crumbs. He used to say 'I'll chop your bloody fingers off in a minute!'
>
> Nellie (born 1916)

> He was dressed just like Mr Pastry, remember Mr Pastry? It was a lock-up shop and he used to come down Nightingale Lane to his shop and he used to have this black suit and shirt with fly collars and his little bow tie and his little bowler hat.
>
> Lizzie (born 1927)

People remembered the haberdasher's, the draper's (who sold coloured ribbon and tapes as well as linen and fabrics), the oil and hardware, paraffin and wood shop, the candle shop, the oat shop, the barber's, the cats' meat shop, the wet fish shop, numerous grocer's, several butcher's, the baker's, the tobacconist, the post office, the Diploma laundry and the delicatessen. There were enamel advertisements on the walls of the corner shops:

Our mother used to send us round for a quarter of ham and they used to do it up so nice – they used to roll it so we couldn't undo it and eat any bringing it home.

Elsie (born 1913)

And Jackson's, you used to go there and get all your nice ham that he'd cut off the bone, and it was beautiful ham with a bit of fat all the way round, and I had a sister and when she used to go and get the ham she'd always have a little pick of it before she got home and my Mum, as soon as she got in, she'd know that Alice had been at it …

Lizzie (born 1927)

The shops stayed open late, usually until about 8pm:

They was good. You never saw 'em with a shutter up. And the lights was on in the winders all night after they'd shut.

Lilly (born 1925)

In the twenties and thirties there were several dairies and cow barns in Wapping which sold fresh milk. Ernie used to feed the cows in the barn at the bottom of his street:

Down Wapping, at the bottom of Malay Street, there used to be a turning called Ship Street and there used to be a cow barn there, and we used to see 'Daddy Winn', [as] we used to call him, the Governor, and he used to let us go in there and with the mangel-wurzels and help to grind them down for the cattle.

Ernie (born 1913)

By the end of the Second World War there were no dairies left. The idea of obtaining milk straight from the cow was alien to children, as Barbara discovered when she came to Wapping:

I used to try and take nature study with them and they simply didn't know what a cow was! Milk came from United Dairies!

Barbara (teacher at St Peter's School, 1949)

Horses and carts were the main form of transport for everything before the Second World War and there were several stables in Wapping. Mary recalled seeing horse-drawn fire engines being used to put out a big fire in Metropolitan Wharf which killed two of the firemen, both friends of her father. Her father had been in charge of one of the stables:

It used to be like a carnival on Sunday because they used to take all the horses out and tie 'em up there and wash them. This chap – he'd have his own horse and another horse and be riding round bare-backed doing all tricks.

Mary (born 1912)

Horses stood in a line along the High Street with their noses in their bags, waiting for their carts to be loaded or unloaded. Many children were fond of feeding the horses and of getting to know them:

It was just a matter of, if you dealt with horses in the street, you'd find that some of them were different, as their carters would say, you know 'this one's alright, nice and quiet, the other one's' … something you couldn't repeat! Bill (born 1926)

On weekdays the pavements were bustling with people going about their daily work, and the roads were jammed with horse-drawn traffic clip-clopping on the cobbles, their carts piled high with goods from the docks. The horse dung was cleared from the streets at 5 p.m. every day:

They used to come round and sweep up the manure and the water cart used to come round of a night time with a spray. They sprayed the water to clean the street more than they do now. We used to run behind the water cart – the water cart came round and cleaned all the horses' pee up.

Ada (born 1909)

George 'Daddy' Winn's cow barn, *c.* 1920. Before the Second World War there were many cow barns in the East End producing milk for the neighbourhood. The legend reads 'Thorley's special cow cake.'

Police stopping a loaded 'van' (horse and cart). (Copyright Museum of London/PLA collection)

On Sundays, however, when the docks were idle, the clatter of horses, men darting about on bicycles and the shouts of workers loading and unloading in the docks were replaced by the sounds of children playing in the streets by the docks without the fear of being knocked down.

The world beyond Wapping could seem very distant: very few people had telephones until after the Second World War. Audrey, whose family did own a telephone, remembers 'half of Wapping' coming in to use it. There had been an Underground station in Wapping since 1869. According to Mary, the steam from the goods trains passing through once came up the air shafts and into people's back yards. The line was electrified in 1913 and amalgamated into the Underground system. Apart from this, however, there was a dearth of public transport in Wapping, no doubt because of the obstruction of the bridges. Most people were used to walking everywhere because travel was difficult and expensive for the average family. The majority rarely travelled out of Wapping. If they did, it was a major expedition:

We used to, of a, say, Easter or Whitsun, we'd go all the way to Farnborough on a horse and cart – that's a long way!

Ernie (born 1913)

In the chapters that follow, old Wappingites themselves will tell more about the inside story of what it was like to live there.

Notes:

1. The London Docks were situated in Wapping and were so named to emphasise their position at the centre of the port. They were closed along with all the other docks except Tilbury following the introduction of container ships which were too large to come upstream into shallow waters.
2. Now Garnet Street
3. There is, however, a degree of ambiguity surrounding the definition of Wapping. From the local's viewpoint Wapping was within the area bounded by the bridges. On the other hand, official boundaries illustrated in a map dating from 1893 show that the area considered by locals to be Wapping is also part of the area covered by the wards of St George in the East and Shadwell. This confusion makes it impossible to obtain accurate demographic statistics for the area which for official purposes, was included with Limehouse and Ratcliffe wards, as part of the London Borough of Stepney.
4. It was closed down in 1981.
5. Meredith and Drew biscuit factory was bombed in the War and replaced by a tower block, Gordon House.
6. A tobacco factory.
7. One of the oldest pubs in London, founded in 1520, frequented by Samuel Pepys, J.M.W. Turner and Charles Dickens. One resident described it as 'a grim old boozer' between the wars.
8. By 1953 this had fallen drastically to a total of ten pubs in the whole of Wapping, source *Ship without Sails* M. Lloyd Turner 1953.
9. Now Bridewell Place.
10. Demolished and replaced in the early sixties by a tower block, Oswell House.
11. St John's Church School was completed around 1760 and still has the picturesque statues of a girl and a boy on its façade.
12. Founded in 1798 to control piracy and lawlessness on the river and still in operation today from the river front in Wapping.
13. In 1961 measures were taken to clean up the river by improving the sewage system and reducing the amounts of industrial waste draining into it.
14. Walter Jones, source *Tender Grace* by Madge Darby.
15. The community still exists at the time of writing.
16. Jack Banfield: born 1907, source: transcript from interview in 1985, Museum in Docklands.
17. It was actually a harmonium.
18. Lascars were Asiatic seamen who first started coming to the East End in the nineteenth century. They were mainly from the Indian subcontinent from Bengal, Ceylon and Burma.
19. According to Jack Banfield, he was 'an African' who had been a ship's cook.

2

HOUSING

Before the slum clearances in the twenties and thirties, most people in Wapping lived in dark, narrow, cobbled, back streets and alleyways in crumbling rented Victorian houses or tenement blocks. Large families were packed into rows of two-storey terraced houses with one room on each floor and a small yard at the back. What was it like growing up in a home like this?

People who had spent their earliest years in these living conditions generally were very matter-of-fact about the overcrowding:

> There were four blocks and I mean they were absolutely crowded – big blocks of tenement buildings
>
> Janet (born 1921)

> They were about three stories and they were all different families in each storey. So you lived downstairs and somebody in the middle and another one up the top and they was all paying rent.
>
> Lilly (born 1925)

There would often be one outside toilet for all the families:

> Well in my house we had Mrs M at the bottom, there was her husband and her husband's brother, then she had six daughters and they lived in the bottom. On our floor, there was myself, my mother, sister – two sisters, my brother and on the top floor there was a relative and her husband and one girl. So count that lot up!
>
> Lilly (born 1925)

This adds up to seventeen people using one toilet:

> But the toilet was kept beautiful. I'm not saying all the street was, but our one was lovely.
>
> Lilly (born 1925)

Dolly's family also shared a toilet in the yard with several other families in an old slum in the 1920s:

> Well, it was clean, there were so many used it – and you tried to clean it, we tried to keep it clean, we were as clean as we could be.
>
> Dolly (born 1912)

The severe shortage of living space and lack of housing affected people at all stages of their lives. Engaged couples, (who invariably had met locally 'down Wapping') would have to put their marriage 'on hold' for years before they could move into a place of their own. Norman and Sal decided to get married even though they could not live together – the opposite, you could say, of 'living in sin!'

> Well we wouldn't have got married would we, only, you was thirty, weren't you, and I was twenty four, and we wanted to get married and we never had nowhere to live, and I said 'How can we get married, we've got nowhere to live?' and he said 'Yeah, we will get married and we'll live apart' and we lived apart for eighteen months before we got a flat. We had our son, didn't we – he was about a year old, wasn't he, when we got

Raymond Street before the slum clearance, *c.* 1929. Janet lived in one of these houses. (Copyright LMA)

the flat. We lived apart for eighteen months before we got a flat. Cos I used to live with my Mum and Norm used to live with his Mum. Weekends we used to be together.

Sal (born 1925)

Many people, like Dolly, were impatient to get married in order to enjoy some privacy and independence:

We lived there – that was in Reigate Street. I always remember I got married from there, thank goodness – good to have a little room and a place of you own innit.

Dolly (born 1912)

This arrangement for a large family was typical:

We had an old fashioned house, two bedrooms up, two bedrooms between ten of us and one downstairs in the kitchen.

Elsie (born 1913)

Smaller families were frequently no better off; Dolly, an only child, shared one room with her mother who was a widow. People had to think of makeshift solutions to maximise the space:

Me and my sister, we used to have a bed settee, and of a night time we used to put the bed down and mornings we used to roll it up.

Nellie (born 1916)

Not only did people have to share rooms, but they also usually had to share beds with their siblings. Lizzie, referring to this, said jokingly:

I can remember – we always say (cos all my family are little) and we say it's cos we slept top and bottom in the bed – you didn't have room to [grow]!

Lizzie (born 1927)

Norman had eight brothers and sisters:

Yeah, well, I think it was two bedrooms, one down and one up, and really the down one was really a living room but things were that bad in them days that they had to make that living room into a bedroom. I know, cos my Mum and Dad used to sleep in their own room and we used to have boarders upstairs and we used to sleep in – I dunno, about four or five in the bed! Up and down, know what I mean, head to toe! Used to be – oh it was very, very poor wasn't it!

Norman (born 1919)

He explained that he had had to share a bed with his sisters:

The parents were always in their own room but we used to sleep where we could really –there was eight children in our family and to tell you the truth, I don't know how we all got in there! [Laughs] There was so much shuffling about, maybe one time you'd be sleeping in a little bed and somebody else might want it, then you'd be sleeping somewhere else. Even with your sisters. Yeah, it wasn't – what would you call it – [pause] well, what could I say? Anyway …

Norman (born 1919)

At least in that family all the children slept under the same roof, which was not something to be taken for granted:

Well, me mother and father, they slept – it was a very narrow room, upstairs it was, and they had a bed going that way and we had a sofa in them days, and we pulled it out and three of us 'd be – Connie and Harry … so the three of us slept on the old sofa. We only had two rooms, as I said, me mother, father and three sons, we lived in the other end, the top room, altogether five in the room, other brothers and sisters they slept in Red Lion Street.

Tom (born 1923)

No matter how cramped the accommodation, for many families it was essential to have a parlour:

Course, all us kids, when we was young, we had two bedrooms upstairs, three bedrooms – one bedroom was taken for the parlour, like.

Elsie (born 1913)

In Tom's family there was no question of turning the parlour into a bedroom so the children could all sleep in the same house:

The parlour was never used. You musn't use that – that's the gospel truth that is! … we weren't allowed in there! Only went in there when they had a couple of parties in there, when me mother and father had their friends … they might have had a bit of a knees up, but apart from that it was locked up.

Tom (born 1923)

Ernie's family unlocked the parlour once a week for Sunday dinner:

We never had a tablecloth on the table – always newspaper. Of a Sunday, you'd have a tablecloth plus table in the parlour.

Ernie (born 1913)

It was a matter of self-respect to have one room in the house which could impress outsiders on important occasions such as engagements, weddings and funerals. Whereas the front door was left open, or the key left on a string behind the letterbox so that any neighbour could pop in and out at any time, the parlour was strictly out of bounds. It contained the household's most prized possessions:

We had a piano – no-one could play it!

Ernie (born 1913)

I remember we had a table in there and a piano …it was never played though … and a mirror and pictures in there and a fire grate.

Tom (born 1923)

This was all of a piece with keeping the steps scrubbed and whitened and the curtains and windows clean. Ethel recalled her row of houses with pride:

… all lovely, decent places, and they always had an aspidistra.

Ethel (born 1916)

Inside, the décor was sombre:

Where they used to have mantelpieces years ago, they used to have vases and clocks and that, and we used to have a drape to go on the mantelpiece, a velvet drape.

Nellie (born 1916)

All bom boms [sic] on them and you always had a guard round it didn't you. It was all dark brown, dark brown paint weren't it, like it weren't bright like it is now.

Lizzie (born 1927)

The houses were cold and draughty and were heated as well as people could manage with fires. Fuel was a major item in the family budget. People from Wapping and beyond would lug large quantities of coke home on barrows and prams for their fires:

There was a gas works down by St Peter's School; we used to go there on a Saturday morning and order twenty eight pounds of coke and we had to be helped carrying it up, but we was thankful for that because we loved the coke.

Ada (born 1909)

Coal was an expensive item for many households so that people tended to use it sparingly in a mixed fire composed of coke, coal and driftwood:

We had lovely fires then, because they used to go down the shore, the boys used to go down there and collect the driftwood, and my Dad used to go down there and get the wood, and he'd get the bigger pieces of wood, and he'd get them down in the yard in Tower Buildings and he'd saw that up, and the boys used to have to chop it as well, but they used to saw it up into small logs so the coke and the wood, the sea-wood, burnt together.

Ada (born 1909)

Often the kitchen was the only room with a fire going, and the whole family would cluster round it, competing for the warmest place:

Me father used to sit right on top of the grate – you couldn't feel the fire – in a great big armchair.

Elsie (born 1913)

… as kids you'd sit in front of the fire, the grate, there's a knock at the door: 'Go on, it's your turn, you open it!' Do you know why? Because when he or she got up, the other one sat in their place!

Ron (born 1921)

The bedrooms were chillier:

It wasn't really too cold because our bedroom backed onto the next door neighbour's fireplace, so we got all their warmth, see.

Ada (born 1909)

In the poorest families people shivered in their beds:

> I've known it where fathers would have to put their coats over as bedding.
>
> Ron (born 1921)

Children could warm up at a church club and fathers often escaped to the pub:

> St Patrick's of an evening, St Peter's had it – they used to have these teachers come down, like gym teachers, yeah and that was somewhere to go and it was warm.
>
> Doris (born 1923)

Most houses were connected to metered gas for cooking and lighting. The gas mantle was very flimsy and kept breaking, and the ceiling was usually black from the soot:

> You'd have to light the mantle ... with a match.
>
> Lilly (born 1925)

During the night people used candles to save money on the gas:

> My Mum always had a night light burning all night. You had a saucer of water and you'd put these night lights in and they lasted eight hours ... it weren't a bright light but, like, you could see ...
>
> Lizzie (born 1927)

Where possible, people avoided using the outside toilet at night:

> It was very creepy of a night if you wanted to go to the loo – although most people had chamber pots in those days.
>
> Norman (born 1919)

He confessed that at least he did not have to empty the chamber pot – that was his mother's job! Dolly had bad memories of using the toilet during the night:

> Well, it was down in the, what we would call the yard, and if you lived in this house there was other people using it which wasn't very nice, but it was in an old house and you used to have to go down, it was dark down there – I always remember going down with a candle.
>
> Dolly (born 1912)

As with many of the poorest people living in Wapping in the 1920s, there was no running water inside the building where Dolly was living:

> You had to keep going down the yard to get water – me mother used to have a nice white jug for water for use in the house to drink.
>
> Dolly (born 1912)

She remembered that there would be a kettle permanently on the stove for tea, but that whenever she needed water, she would have to fill a bucket from the outside tap and haul it up several flights of stairs to heat it up on the gas. Other people heated their water in a copper which they kept in the yard. They filled it with cold water from the outside tap and heated it up on the fire.

These conditions account for the experiences of the majority of people living in Wapping before the slum clearances. There were, of course, those who lived in comparative luxury. Annie's family, who had a holiday house in Essex, moved into Wapping when a new block of spacious flats with lifts was built in 1928.[1]

During the twenties and thirties, the London County Council initiated a programme of slum clearance throughout the capital. Many people moved out to satellite suburbs in Essex and Kent sometimes referred to as 'Little Wapping.'[2] The people who were rehoused in Wapping during the slum clearances all knew people who had moved out. Generally they were not envious of them.

Above left: Jubilee Buildings, 1949. This photograph was originally published in *Picture Post* with the title 'The slums of Wapping'. Barbara remembered local people being offended by the article. The boys have been collecting firewood. (Copyright Getty Images)

Above right: Pearl Street looking west, 1938. In the background is St George's Hospital. St Peter's School is on the right. (Copyright Tower Hamlets Local History Library)

At one time they always used to go to Dagenham – used to call it 'corned beef city' … we're going back again to the early thirties and the rents there was a bit dearer, and they paid their fare to get to London or anywhere and of course, they found out that they could hardly afford it and all they could live on was corned beef!

Janet (born 1921)

Well, I was only a kid at the time – we used to say. 'They've gone down to Dagenham – kippers and custard!' Well, they'd gone down there and how are they going to afford to buy the furniture and all that down there? They had a house down there – up here you was sharing rooms and that was the expression 'kippers and custard'.

Ron (born 1921)

In 1934 the Labour Party, under the leadership of Herbert Morrison, gained control of the majority of the London Borough councils and made the slum clearances a top priority. They set about demolishing many of the backstreets, courtyards and alleyways, sweeping away corner shops and other neighbourhood meeting places where people stopped to chat as they went about their daily business. Annie Barnes was a member of the Stepney Housing Committee during this period. She described the fury of some Wapping people living in the worst conditions, at the prospect of the destruction of their homes and neighbourhood:

Anyway, we on the housing committee sent out special inspectors and they reported back to us, and it seemed that a place called Wapping Wall by the river was one of the worst places. A few of us went along there with the architect and the borough engineer, and as we approached they came out like savages. They came with broomsticks, even choppers. Talk about Dickens! We had to have nearly all the police from Shadwell Station to protect us but we managed to have a good look round. They had no back yards, just little passages, and they were in a terrible state. They didn't have water. I don't know how they managed.

They just went on shouting, 'It was good enough for our grandmothers. It's good enough for us. Go away! Just get rid of the rats. We're alright here, if you'd just get rid of the rats!'

Extract from *From Suffragette to Stepney Councillor:*
Tough Annie Barnes in Conversation with Kate Harding and Caroline Gibbs, (Stepney books, 1980)

It seems that the council took some notice of this outcry. November 4-9 1935 was designated 'National Rat Week'. The council employed three full-time rat catchers to place bait laced with rat poison in the sewers.[3]

In 1932 the London County Council built a large new estate to replace the rows of little terraced houses and derelict buildings and many of the remaining streets were renamed. The new blocks of flats were all named after famous seamen, voyagers and discoverers who had sailed from Wapping.[4] All dwellings were to have a bath, gas-fired coppers, heaters, cookers and gas lighting. Dolly, when she was living in the one room with her mother, watched the construction of the new flats opposite her tenement building:

I always used to say to my mother. 'Ooh they look lovely, are we going into those nice new flats?' 'Oh no,' she said, 'I can't afford the rent o' them'. I said. 'It'd be lovely' cos they had bathrooms and everything.

Dolly (born 1912)

There was, in actual fact, no room dedicated as a bathroom in those flats at that time:

In those days in Willoughby House, the two-bedroom flats, the bath was in the scullery with the lid on, so anyone having a bath – no-one could go in and cook or anything! Had to time it that no-one wanted to go into the kitchen – we called it 'the scullery.'

Janet (born 1921)

At Christmas Lizzie's family would cover the bath lid with a baize tablecloth so that they could eat their Christmas dinner off it. The council proudly announced the improved facilities for the residents of the new estate. People in council housing remembered having to abide by a long list of rules and regulations:

They used to have a washing line, you were not allowed to put that up before ten o'clock in the morning, put it down at eight o'clock at night and no ball games.

Ron (born 1921)

Electricity was not universal until as late as 1950. It is difficult to imagine the excitement people felt at the prospect of moving into a flat with electricity, and modern sanitation:

I was fourteen in September when the War began, and by then we'd just moved over to Matilda House, we'd got new flats. We didn't realise what it was to switch the light on and off!

Lilly (born 1925)

It was like a *palace* moving in there – because you had the bathroom and separate toilet, didn't we, and electric light!

Sal (born 1925)

This was the last generation which could not take heating, electricity, inside sanitation and running water for granted.

Notes

1. Riverside Mansions.
2. Patrick Hanshaw, *All My Yesterdays*. See the well-known study *Family and Kinship in East London* by Michael Young and Peter Willmott, first published in 1957.
3. Source: Public Health report 1935 for the Borough of Stepney.
4. 'The Wapping Housing Estate 1932', from *The Co-partnership Herald*, Vol. 11, No. 21 (November 1932).

3

THE FAMILY

During the 1920s and 1930s, life for ordinary working-class people revolved around the family. Large families were the norm, and people regarded six or seven children as average. Elsie, who had nine sisters, remembered being teased by her teacher:

> My Mum had all hers at home, cos the teacher used to say, 'You'll have another new baby when you get home!' I suppose my Dad said 'We'll try for a boy', but she was unlucky, no, ten girls.
>
> Elsie (born 1913)

In such large families, the children were from different generations. Ted recalled a particularly large family:

> Sixteen children! ... and funny enough, her younger son, Dave, his older sister had children older than him and yet they had to call him 'Uncle'.
>
> Ted (born 1926)

Often siblings hardly knew each other because of the age gap. Janet was thirteenth in a family of fourteen:

> My oldest brother who I hadn't seen then, he was in the army in India, even when we were born, the younger ones. And me oldest sister, I think she went into service or something, in Berkshire.
>
> Janet (born 1921)

Many mothers relied on their older children for help. Lizzie was one of the youngest of the family:

> Me being the twelfth one of all those children, I benefited more than the older ones ... see the older ones going a work [sic] and bringing the money, and your mother had more money to spend ... you'd take a big bottle of water, and you'd go over the park, and the older ones used to have to watch the little ones.
>
> Lizzie (born 1927)

Since so many babies died at birth or in infancy, people often lost track of how many brothers and sisters they actually had. The whole subject was somewhat taboo. A mother could not feel secure about the survival of her child past early childhood, especially if it was a boy. Mary's mother followed the centuries-old custom of dressing her boys in girls' clothing until she felt that they were out of danger. Tragically, only one boy survived:

> I don't know how many Mum had altogether but we was left with one brother. Well, I think some of them Mum lost at birth and I had another young brother, but she said she could not ever rear one past the age of five – boys – why, I don't know.
>
> Mary (born 1912)

When Mary had her own son in the 1930s, she must have feared that he too would not survive. Nevertheless she flouted the tradition of her mother's generation:

Above: Mothers and children. This photograph was taken in 1921 outside New Tower Buildings. There are five mothers and twenty-six children.

Right: Two sisters, 1926. Children from the same family often spanned two generations.

Mother with baby boy. This picture was taken around 1905. The male infant is dressed in girl's clothing as was the custom at that time. It was also usual not to cut boys' hair when they were babies.

… when he was younger I used to make all his things – the Hungarian shirts. He used to have long golden curls, he used to have black satin trousers, always white boots and socks … I always swore that I'd never put a boy in dresses when he was born and I never did … well, years ago, most of the boys, I think, was put in dresses when they was first born … even when my son was small, some of them, and I always said I'd never put him in dresses and as luck would have it, I had him, and he never went in a dress.

Mary (born 1912)

People's parents had been brought up during the reign of Queen Victoria – Mary's grandparents had actually worked for her as nurse and gardener – and many of them held attitudes typical of that era; fathers tended to be strict, mothers more lenient:

I mean, you had to mind your p's and q's when you was sitting round the table. Well if you said something like 'I got free of them, Dad', and he said 'What did you say?' 'I said *three.*' You had to sound your 'h's' but you used to forget after that, but he'd pull you up about anything like that.

Norman (born 1919)

More than one docker's child remembered their father's fastidiousness about his clothes. In Janet's family, the children took it in turns to polish their father's boots before he went to work in the docks. Norman remembered being sent out to collect his father's shirt dicky fronts and collars from the cleaners. He and his wife, Sal, recalled how Norman's father dressed to go to work:

Well he wore just ordinary clothes, not an overall or anything like that, just his suit. He was smart, my Dad … and he used to wear the old cap and tie. A scarf, cotton or silk. All colours. He wouldn't wear a white one – no way! But he was very smart, my old Dad. They used to call him 'the clerk of the works', his other brothers, because he was smarter than them.

Norman (born 1919), Sal (born 1925)

Ethel's father wore a bowler hat on special occasions:

> [Her mother] bought him a lovely bowler hat , steamed it, washed it, steamed it all up so' it would shine. You know he was very smart …
>
> Ethel (born 1916)

If anything, women paid less attention to their appearance than men:

> The Mums, if you saw them they would always have these great wrap around pinafores that did up behind, you know. And that was the sort of typical thing.
>
> Barbara (teacher at St Peter's School in 1949)

The older women sometimes wore a cap and shawl, and long skirts reaching down to their ankles. Jack remembered his grandmother fondly:

> She was a lovely lady – always in with my mother with a big apron, you know, white aprons.
>
> Jack (born 1924)

Most people thought the world of their mother, and some could not talk about her without becoming very emotional. They looked back on her with a painful mixture of warmth, gratitude and compassion, for the all the years of relentless hard work she had endured to keep the family going. Several people referred to their mother as 'my poor mother', or 'poor thing'. This comment from Lizzie was typical:

> She was a *wonderful* mother! Yeah, they were, they worked hard, they looked old really, when you think back.
>
> Lizzie (born 1927)

Tom was full of regret that he had not appreciated his mother more:

> Oh if only she was alive today what wouldn't I do for her!
>
> Tom (born 1923)

Jack admired his mother's belligerence. Having no father, he felt he needed to protect the rest of the family.

> When I was a boy I used to look after my sisters, you know what I mean. I was the man of the house … I was always quick-tempered, very quick with me hands. I had to be, I mean, I had sisters and my mother always said 'If anyone hits you, you hit 'em back and if they hit you again you hit 'em twice and if they hit you twice you hit 'em back four times'.
>
> Jack (born 1924)

Mary attributed almost mythical powers to her mother, who also was quick to use her fists to defend any member of her family in a dispute:

> Our mother had all the strength in her hair. She could swing anyone round on her hair and it wouldn't bother her.
>
> Mary (born 1912)

She followed her mother's example when it came to sticking up for her younger brother:

> If any boys bigger than him started on him round here, I'd be in there! Mum used to say to me 'You're going to get yourself into trouble', cos I was only at school at the time, but no one could take a liberty with him cos he was smaller than them.
>
> Mary (born 1912)

Fathers and mothers generally had very clearly defined roles. The father was the breadwinner and the head of the household. The mother ran the home and looked after the children. Providing food was not something to be taken for granted. Although Ada did not have a good relationship with her father, she was thankful to be fed:

> He always foraged for us though he was an old so-and-so, he was.
>
> Ada (born 1909)

Norman was similarly grateful to his father:

> One thing he did was to see that we had plenty to eat. He was good that way.
>
> Norman (born 1919)

In some families, the father enjoyed special privileges – the seat in front of the fire, or a chop with the kidney on it when the rest of the family were having stew. Mary's father did not quite fit with the stereotype:

> My Dad would make a lovely Christmas pudding. The only thing, if you had a piece of it you'd get drunk! He used to put *everythink* in it!
>
> Mary (born 1912)

He made big puddings which he boiled in his gas-fired copper. This was also used to heat up water for washing horses.

Most dockers stopped off for a drink in the pub on the way home from work. With Janet's father, one drink led to another, and this caused problems:

> I can remember we had to get out of our father's way when he came home. By the time he came home from the docks and had had a drink and all that, his dinner had to be there on the table, separate, none of us dared do any playing about 'til he finished.
>
> Janet (born 1921)

Mothers and daughters were very caught up in each others' lives. This involvement, extensively described in the classic book *Family and Kinship in East London* was equally strong in Wapping. When a young woman had left home, got married and had her own family, she would very likely be seeing more of her mother than her husband, just as her mother had done with her grandmother. She would see her Mum every day or even several times a day – especially if she only lived round the corner, sharing chores and all the ups and downs of daily life. Sometimes a woman's Mum moved in to look after the children. Kathleen and her mother shared both their cleaning job and the childcare, covering for each other both at home and at work when necessary. Meanwhile, most men were in their own separate world – usually working in the docks.

Many people would go to any lengths to help their parents when they had grown old and infirm. Lizzie described how she and her sisters used to look after their father after their mother had died:

> And we used to go up, me and my sister, once a week, and we done all his cleaning, and then my [other] sister always kept his winders clean and my [other sister] used to get his shopping and all that. And that's how people were, weren't they, like you never had home helps.
>
> Lizzie (born 1927)

People often took their parents into their own household as a matter of filial duty. This could, of course, lead to tensions between the generations, especially when a mother-in-law moved in.

As a rule, people were surrounded by relatives:

> There was my mother's brother next door, there was my other mother's brother next door to him, there was Uncle Johnny, Uncle Dan, me mother and me nan next door.
>
> Ethel (born 1916)

If relations were not next door or in the next street, they were mostly within walking distance:

Three generations. Grandmother, mother and daughter all living in Wapping.

I had relatives up at Limehouse at Salmon's Lane, you know – that was miles away at the time' and I'd go and see Aunt Rose and Aunt Kate – they were very good to me: 'cup of tea or lemonade or cake?'

Bill (born 1926)

With so many relatives to visit, especially on Sundays, who needed any other social life?

Small families were usually small for a good reason. Perhaps the father had died in the First World War, or was abroad serving in the Merchant Navy. Lilly had never met her father:

Well, to be honest, I never had one [a father]. I was illegitimate – my sister and I, because my mother's first husband was killed in the war and she had two children and unfortunately she got mixed up with someone, and my sister and I was the consequence.

Lilly (born 1925)

These matters were never mentioned within the family. Lilly naturally thought this was a normal state of affairs until she went to school:

I realised later on at school – all the others had fathers, but I never. And do you know, from the day I was born 'til now, I never ever asked my mother who he was, why, or anything else, and nor did my sister!

Lilly (born 1925)

There were secrets in Doris' family too:

My mother only had me and a sister that's older than me and apparently had had a son which I never knew about ... In those days they never told anything.

Doris (born 1923)

Single mothers had to go out to work to earn some money. They were forced to lean heavily on relatives to help out with the children. Relatives also gave money if they had any to spare:

> My father died of war wounds. He fought in the Dardanelles, he died for the 1914 War and my mother was carrying me and my father dropped dead having dinner.[2] They were quite a big family and my mother went to work at St George's hospital, which was in Wapping, as a cleaner. My Gran brought us up, my Grandma, you know, as she done with all the family ... they took two of my sisters away to Somerset but my mother had 'em back, because she went to work.
>
> Jack (born 1924)

Lilly's mother found a job in a nearby sack factory:

> Well, there was a big family and they all lived in the street and my eldest aunt, she used to provide three of us with a dinner everyday.
>
> Lilly (born 1925)

Dolly's mother, a First World War widow who also worked in a sack-repairing factory, got by with the help of her mother and sister. Doris' mother actually moved house in order to help her sister:

> My aunt married about seventeen ... and she wanted my mother down because she had so many kids – and so my mother helped to bring them up – she had thirteen, my aunt.
>
> Doris (born 1923)

The concept of 'the family' was very flexible. Just as parents and grandparents, uncles and aunts, frequently came to live with the younger generation when they were old and frail, families took in children in need, rather than see them sent into an institution. For some people there was not much difference between relatives and close friends – they all became part of the family:

> Well we had a lot of aunts and my Mum, I mean she lost *the equivalent of another sister* with the flu.
>
> Jack (born 1924)

If all the members of one family met up for a celebration, it could be quite a crowd!

> Even to this day all the children are still all friendly, we all meet now and again, and Nellie was eighty, six years ago, and they gave her a surprise party ... her family, with her children, her in-laws and all her grandchildren came to one hundred people!
>
> Lizzie (born 1927)

Most people could count on the loyalty and sense of duty of their families when they ran into difficulties. For those without this safety net, the alternatives were frightening: destitution or surrender to the mercies of the state. Janet had had a difficult life from the beginning; her parents had muddled along with 'their ups and downs' and both died when she was only an adolescent, whereupon her older siblings threw her onto the street:

> Well, you know, I think it was one of them things – some people had big families and couldn't keep them.
>
> Ted (born 1926)

> Me relations – their father got killed in the [First World] War. Well the women couldn't look after 'em and they got put in Barnado's and they shipped them out to New Zealand and Australia and Canada but my mother never wanted to do that with us, no way.
>
> Jack (born 1924)

Doris mentioned that during the first years of the twentieth century there were notices in Watney Market inviting people to claim abandoned children before they were sent to Canada.[3] Mary's mother had taken pity on a little boy in the neighbourhood who had suffered terrible neglect because of his father's alcoholism:

He had three sisters and a brother, and Mum used to keep buying them shoes and that. She took him because he was only about six weeks old. People used to come and say that they were sitting under arches with no shoes and socks and crying, his brothers and sisters.

Mary (born 1912)

Ellen Kemp, who grew up in Wapping in the thirties and died in 1998, had the most miserable and deprived of childhoods, thanks to her violent, alcoholic father.[4] She and her sister felt such wonderful relief when they were taken into a Dr Barnado's home in Woodford, where they were treated with kindness for the first time. Sadly, this did not last long. Soon after, she was transferred to another children's home, where she fell into the hands of the sadistic nun in charge. In those days little thought was given to protecting children from abusive adults.

Ethel had had a friend who took in an abandoned baby. She saw the infant lying on steps of the Barnado's children's home in Stepney one day when she was walking past:

... coming home they found the baby on the doorstep, and she brought him home and she brought that boy up 'til he went to the war. He was the most beautiful boy that they said you could ever see, and Emily's Mum told me that he went into the army and got killed. *Got killed!* She was so upset, she'd brought him up from a baby.

Ethel (born 1916)

She never made any attempt to find out where the child came from, as he clearly was not wanted, and she knew that by taking him in, she was quite likely to be saving him from forced migration.

Within a generation, family life was to change dramatically. One of the major transformations resulting from the Second World War was the increased participation of women in the world of work. The rise in the status of women, and a general improvement in economic security led to a sharp fall in the number of babies they had. With the smaller family unit, the days of desperate fear of destitution were soon to become history.

Notes

1. It was approximately 1½ miles away.
2. The timing of Jack's father's death is a little confusing. Jack's father was wounded in the First World War and died suddenly when Jack was two when the family were having dinner as a delayed consequence of his war wounds.
3. Canada was the first country that children were sent to from Barnado's homes. After 1921 children were sent to Australia as well. The first party of girls were received in Australia under the condition that they worked as domestic staff for at least two years on arrival. Before 1926 adoption was an informal matter and not a legal process. It was often arranged via local newspapers. The natural mother would advertise the child and pay the adoptive parents either a weekly or a lump sum.
4. Source, her autobiography *Don't Let Them See You Cry*, Ellen Kemp. An extract is published in *Rising East* Vol. 3 No. 3.

4

MEN AND WORK

For the vast majority of men living in Wapping, work was related in some way to the docks. There were three main types of river worker: dockers, stevedores and lightermen. Stevedores (originally called 'lumpers' in the nineteenth century) loaded and unloaded ships. Once the cargo was ashore, dockers took over and transported it in and out of warehouses. Lightermen were originally so called because their barges or 'lighters' took cargo from a ship, making it lighter. Dockers and stevedores were not so much differentiated by their work between the two World Wars, as by their unions. Dockers were also sometimes referred to as 'whites' and stevedores 'blues' because of the colour of their union cards. Typically sons went into the same work as their fathers and in many families all the men did the same work for generations. In the hierarchy of river workers, lightermen were considered the elite, followed by stevedores and then dockers. Jack was proud to be a stevedore:

> See, a stevedore was – how can I put it – a *gentleman*. Stevedores loaded ships, dockers unloaded ships … well, I was a stevedore and my father was a stevedore and my grandfather was a stevedore and it was in the family. And automatically I thought I had to be a stevedore.
>
> Jack (born 1924)

It was practically impossible for a man to join the union unless he already had a family connection:

> If your father wasn't a stevedore, no way. Unless they run out of membership, then they started taking son-in-laws. But before they all come in, you had to have a birth certificate to say your father was a stevedore.
>
> Jack (born 1924)

Effectively there was a closed shop which had been established by the close-knit Irish community:

> If you never went to mass you never got a job – that's how it was, you know what I mean! … It was mostly originated that people from the Old Country started it: they built the dock, they dug the dock out, then they started work as stevedores, but mostly it was 80 per cent Catholics …
>
> Jack (born 1924)

Lightermen or bargeman were regarded as the most skilled of all river workers – some people referred to them as 'the kings of the river'. They had to do an apprenticeship for seven years before they could work independently. In order to get their licence, they had to pass a stiff exam for which much swotting was necessary: they had to know the depth of the river at every turn and also master its topography – rather like a black cab driver learning 'the knowledge'.

Boys were normally apprenticed to their fathers. George, a Wapping resident, married into a family of lightermen. His wife's grandfather had brought the first barge into Shadwell basin in 1832. Ted's father was a 'roadsman' – a lighterman who managed stationary barges. So Ted had the opportunity to be apprenticed to his father but he chose to be a docker:

> I entered a pact: you couldn't get a ticket unless you had people working in the docks being dockers. And two of them tried to stop me because my father was a lighterman.

Norman's grandfather wearing Doggett's coat and badge. Thomas Doggett gave his name to an annual rowing race for watermen on the Thames, which he started in 1715. It still takes place today. The prize is a traditional waterman's red coat with a silver badge and a cash sum. Norman's grandfather won the race and Norman's great-grandfather also won it before him.

Well, apprentice lighterman was 12/6d per week but I was getting – as an ordinary boy doing the old monkey mixing – as it was, I was getting 30 shillings, and you're not going to downgrade yourself, but in the long run I should have been a lighterman, but then my father apprenticed me brother's boys – apprenticed one, and then once he'd come of age he could 'prentice his own brother.

Ted (born 1926)

Men were not allowed to work on the river until they were eighteen years of age, and had to wait until they were twenty-one before they could obtain their union 'ticket'. Between leaving school at fourteen and starting work in the docks, they bided their time doing alternative work – usually jobs in small local factories. To register, a man had to join a union – either the Stevedores Union or the Transport and General Workers' Union. After working continuously in the industry for a minimum of six months, he had to appear in front of a joint committee consisting of employers and union officials in order to become a registered member. He was then given a brass tally with his union membership number on it. The point of this was to control the number of men working in the docks and to ensure that they were suitable for the work.

Until the late 1930s most dock workers were casual, which meant that they were paid by the hour for piece work. The foreman would throw a brass bit into the crowd of men who, in times of extreme hardship, would actually fight over it in order to get work. This struggle was born out of a very real fear of starvation.[1] First thing in the morning, a docker would have to join the throng of fellow-workers at the dock gate, all competing with each other for work:

The call used to be quarter to eight of a morning and then if you got no work you went again at a quarter to one in the afternoon … according to the tide. I remember as a kid, playing in the street, all of a sudden one of the fathers would come out and say to Johnny Jones, 'Johnny, go up the gate and see how many's wanted!'

Ron (born 1921)

The foreman from the ship selected the men for work, choosing either people he knew already, or men who he favoured for some other reason. Registered men who could produce a union card to prove they were up to date with their membership payments took precedence over 'nonners' – the unregistered men:

Some of the dockers round here, prior to the National Dock Labour Board years ago, used to be took on for an hour's work and paid sixpence – it was really very hard.

Jack (born 1924)

The decision as to whether a man was selected for work or not often seemed arbitrary:

There were men who would do ten times the work but they never got a job.

Jack (born 1924)

Tom started work in the docks in the 1940s. He remembered how dreadful he felt when he was left standing on the stones:

It was – I'm trying to think of the word – it was – not embarrassing but belittling, it was *belittling*. The foreman would come out and he would get you called off the stones. You all lined up on the pavement, on the kerbstones and the foreman would come out and – say there was, for example, thirteen men and he might want two gangs, twelve to thirteen men, and he'd come out and select, you know, 'You, you, you', and if your face didn't fit then he'd go past you and go to someone else. Very hard, very embarrassing. I mean I've been on the stones and I've been the last man on the stones – you know, all the others went to work and I was the only man out. You know, if the ground had opened up I wished I'd have dropped in it.

Tom (born 1923)

Norman explained why he decided not to follow his father and brothers into the docks:

I could have gone in the dock because me Dad could have handed it down. I was a bit older than me younger brother, and I could have been the first, but I didn't – I'd seen enough of it, you know. When they was on the pavement they had to be called on, and I was only little, and I'd have had no chance with being called on.

Norman (born 1919)

Some men resorted to ingratiating themselves with the foreman in order to avoid being left 'standing on the stones'. Janet remembered that her father went to the pub after work every evening to 'treat the governor so he would get called on tomorrow.'

Getting called on, or 'shaping up for work' became easier once a man was recognised as a good worker. Most men would try to work for the same company in order to get known. This was called 'piping':

I piped for such and such a firm – 'Scruttons' ... that was the termination used, yeah – 'Where do you work' 'I pipe down at so and so and so and so'. [2]

Tom (born 1923).

The ship's foreman would choose a 'ganger' who worked with a regular group of men or 'gang'.

The foreman, they're called the ship workers, they got to know you ... and at the finish before we became regular, he called us off with the gang ... some ships want thirteen men, that's with deep sea ships, and the short sea trader had twelve men ... we had the same gang of workforce for years, you know.

Tom (born 1923)

This was another reason which made Norman decide against working as a docker:

You had to be in the know as well to get in the dock, because more or less, they were all friendly, you know what I mean. They used to be in little gangs as well, so they wouldn't pick you if you were small, so I said 'No'.

Norman (born 1919)

The sheer variety of goods handled by dockers was astonishing. Tom worked in the London Docks at Wapping, and also at the West India, Victoria, Albert and Tilbury Docks:

You had every commodity under the sun: I mean you might do a job with cement – you might do three hundred ton of cement, you might do three hundred ton of sugar – I'm putting out all the hard jobs, you know.

Cement was hundred weight bags and you was literally picking hundred weight up ... we done a job, it was a back-breaking job, the ship, it was high in the water, so it was coming off a particular run and going out to Canada, but they wanted ballast in the ship to put the ship down a bit. Well, we done them cobblestones, you know, on the road, and there was this shock into the barge and I was working in the barge at the time – oh! it was terrible, and that had to be stowed. It was hard work both ways, you know down at the Albert. But that was only one out of a thousand jobs.

Tom (born 1923)

There were the iron boats at Free Trade Wharf, bringing rails from Middlesborough, which were then unloaded from boats into barges and put onto ships going to Australia and New Zealand. There were the Guinness boats which came to Wapping from Dublin, bringing Guinness and dairy produce. Cork from Portugal came on the Currie boats to the London Docks. Tea, coffee and spices were shifted from warehouses and loaded onto horses and carts. Tom also worked in a tea warehouse in the 1940s:

It was dusty. Would you believe it, when they used to tare – what they called 'tare' empty tea chests. You know what the old tea chests looked like? Well they use to put a bit of canvas down, empty the tea out on there, weigh the tea chest, then you had to put it back. Then you had to do – some did, I didn't – you had to do tea treading – press the tea down.

Tom (born 1923)

This, he explained, was done without taking shoes off! Afterwards the weight was stencilled on:

You'd be surprised how much tea that came out of one of them boxes, you know! Yeah, amazing!

Tom (born 1923)

Dust apart, working in tea warehouses was regarded as one of the easier jobs which could be done in a new suit if the worker wished. 'Boring and bunging' consisted of drilling a hole in a tea chest for the tester to obtain a sample, and then bunging the hole. On the other hand, there were some very dirty jobs:

If you done a dirty commodity like lamp black, now that was filthy, you know. You sweated and that would get in your skin and it would take three days before it would come out – don't matter if you had a bath two hours a day – embedded in your skin.

Tom (born 1923)

Before the use of container ships (from the 1960s onwards) and the consequent demise of the docks, goods were loaded and unloaded mainly by hand:

Men working in the spice factory inspecting cinnamon. (Copyright Museum of London/PLA collection)

41

Everything was manhandled … there was the one item box of tomaters, box of apples, bag of cement – but now, not today – it's all palletised.

Ron (born 1921)

Although electric bogies were in use before the Second World War, forklift trucks were only introduced in the early 1950s:

Really the dock workers were considered like almost the scum of the earth sort of thing – anyone done those sort of jobs – well that was the days when they had to *carry* everything out of the ship's hold.

Victor (born 1930)

You needed strength and stamina to do the many physically exhausting jobs in the docks. George, not a docker himself, described it as 'slavery'. Working with iron and copper 'pencils' or strips, was a good example of this:

This iron was what we called 'shot' in the barges. [It would go] anywhere, you know, sticking up and all intertwined and you had to pull that out. You know, they was jobs that got on your nerves really.

Tom (born 1923)

Some jobs were downright objectionable:

The only worst thing I worked on was down the West and that was fish meal.[3] 'Oh!' my children used to say, 'Mum he's working on fishmeal!' and I always used to have to undress on the balcony. I only had me pants on. But little did they know, they used to give you overalls. Because I was a big man, I could never get any to fit me so I used to have to go out to the shop and buy denims. We used to take nearly two hours to wash and to get it out because as you work you sweat, and it seemed like the fish meal got into the pores and by heck did it smell!

Ted (born 1926)

Then, when he went home from Mile End to Wapping on the train:

Even after I used 'Right Guard' (you know, deodorant), the train's been packed and what with the heat and all of a sudden you see that you're standing on your own, nobody come near you!

Ted (born 1926)

A docker prized his hook, an implement, usually 'S' shaped with a wooden handle, which he used to pick up cases and sacks. Hooks came in various shapes and sizes:

We always used to carry our hooks in our belts you know, cos if you didn't do that you'd probably leave it on a string and forget about it. They used to carry it there, nice and handy. I give mine away … I should have kept it really as a momentum [sic].

Tom (born 1923)

Many goods had to be lifted with cranes or sometimes were shifted using nets and the stakes were very high if anything went wrong. Some materials, such as cement, had to be moved with a special sling and ropes. All this required expertise:

It takes skill to load a ship. If you don't load a ship properly, she'll turn over – that's how ships sink … I liked loading a ship – it's a high loading a ship, I mean fitting twenty ton aboard, a locomotive on board a ship down away to Canada … and using the gear … all the equipment that had to be rigged. And you don't learn it in five minutes.

Jack (born 1924)

Good communication within the gang or team was vital. Ron described how a thirteen-handed gang worked together:

There'd be the top man, the man on the top of the ship on the deck, instructing the winch drivers how to go down and where to place the winch. There're six down holders, they're down the ship's hold, pulling the ropes – they never had nets – they put 'em in ropes, and the four barge hands. One thirteen-handed gang of men done anything say, from five hundred ton to five and a half. And do you know who the greatest feller there was? The representative of the firm, and he was the cheer leader wasn't he.

Ron (born 1921)

The 'cheer leader' chivvied the men to compete with other gangs to make his gang work faster and earn more.

The top man and the crane driver communicated using hand signals. Sidney Bell learnt to drive a crane in six weeks and worked in New Crane Wharf in Wapping handling cocoa, peat from Ireland, tin, tea, rubber and coffee, picking up grain which arrived by barge and transferring it into a hopper.[4] He remembered the lonely responsibility of his crane driving days:

You've got to have your eyes everywhere because you've got to watch that ship. You've got to watch the top man all the time because if he makes a bloomer, you make a bloomer.

Sidney Bell (born 1906)

Everybody had to concentrate so as not to let his colleagues down:

You had to work in a team, don't matter if you was in the warehouses, it was all teamwork, you know. You couldn't say you'd get a job on your own. I wish I could have done because I'm sure I could have earned more money than some of the lazy so and so's who worked with me. There were always people skiving looking for an easy way out.

Tom (born 1923)

Jack, on the other hand, had nothing but admiration for his colleagues:

Take it from me, there's some shrewd people in the dock. You know that it's a college being in the dock, because there's always somebody done something: there's a mechanic in your gang ... there's a builder. There's always an engineer who's always wanted to come into the dock because the money was there. And all those occupations. And in your gang, in my gang I had five or six people who were experts at everything! Builders, electricians, you see [if] I wanted someone to look at something [they'd say] 'I'll be round tonight'.

Jack (born 1924)

He emphasised the close bonds between the men working together:

You had brilliant people and you had what you call friendship. You knew everybody – everybody was your friend. You were in trouble: 'What's the trouble?' and always if you wanted any help, it was there. You know what I mean, if they had a fag they give you half. That's how it was. You'll never believe it, it was a wonderful life, you know what I mean.

(Jack born 1924)

If a docker got into trouble, colleagues would stand up for him. Many of the men had grown up and played together as children. Jack remembered a time when a friend and colleague had got him out of an embarrassing situation with the boss, which otherwise would have cost him his job. The friend had said 'Don't worry about it. I used to copy off you at school didn't I! You always got the cane for that!'

Men valued the variety of the work:

If you was a fitter you'd just be that one job all the time, but you'd be loading the ship, you'd be discharging the ship, you'd be working in the barge, you'd be delivering the goods to load, so you alternated on all different jobs, so you know, it was a pleasure sometimes to go to work.

Ted (born 1926)

Jack made the most of any perks that came his way which, for him, compensated for the harshness of the working conditions:

I used to drink, I mean don't get me wrong, we used to be loading to Iran, Iraq and the Gulf states – could be smoked salmon – all the best, you know what I mean, whatever they had, we had, and in the gear shed we'd always have a drink – we always had something that fall off the back of a lorry.

Jack (born 1924)

It was well known that pilfering from the docks was very widespread:

Mostly the people who lived in Wapping – eight out of ten, I 'spose – was dockers, and they all worked in the docks and they all was thieves!

Eric (born 1913)

Eric himself had not followed his father into the docks. The penalty for pilfering was stiff and some people were still reluctant to discuss this matter. Local newspapers regularly reported thefts by dockers; a typical example was a man who had been caught stealing tea from Colonial Wharf in 1939.[5] The quantity of tea was small enough to slip into his jacket pocket. He was sentenced to a month in custody or a £10 fine. In the same year, a Wapping grocer received 4lb of tea which had been stolen from Colonial Wharf. This was valued at 4s. He was sentenced to six months hard labour.

The docks were kept under surveillance by up to 1,000 uniformed and plain-clothes policemen who could search suspects on demand. Jack was unimpressed by their tactics:

Sometimes they'd try and put a copper in, you know, like underclothes [ie plain clothes]. Well, you knew all along that he was the Bill because of the way you knew one another.

Jack (born 1924)

He and his fellow-workers succeeded in outwitting the police by hiding away castor oil containers filled with whisky. He hinted that he knew about more serious crime in the docks – organised theft on a larger scale than the everyday extras smuggled out by the individual docker to prevent the family from going hungry:

You'd never believe it, when you talk about stuff that would come out of the dock. It would come out in the dust cart, stacked in the middle of other stuff … there was always money to be made!

Jack (born 1924)

Dockers enjoyed their own unique culture, language and way of looking at life. This was known as 'dockology'. There were terms to describe situations peculiar to dock work: loading a ship was referred to as being 'in the slave', a 'top Johnny in a side' was the leader of a gang, a young newcomer was called 'a jazzer', and 'a greenacre' was a load falling from a crane and breaking free in all directions. Dockers went in for nicknames – a very large man weighing more than twenty stone was called 'cuddles':

In the docks, see, everyone has a name. If you got long sideboards they call you 'furniture face' and two brothers, one with a moustache and one without a moustache, they call 'em 'with' and 'without'. …The governor of the CID was a man called 'baby face' – he was an ugly bastard – face a mother couldn't love.

Jack (born 1924)

The camaraderie and shared difficulties bred their own type of humour:

It was hard but it was jovial, I mean you could have a laugh with one another and have a little, what they call 'a chip' – you know – having a go at someone.

Tom (born 1923)

Tom went on to describe a dangerous incident whilst he working with sugar. He saw his colleague's hook handle getting caught on the crane rope:

Well, as the crane took the empty rope up, the rope had caught on the handle of his hook and ripped up his backside and – oh, blimey! – he had the presence of mind as the hook was going up his back, he had the presence of mind to get hold of the rope, you know, so anyway, one of the boys, he shouted up 'Jim', he says 'You're in the pantomime as Peter Pan!' – see that was – you laugh – that was the attitude, you know.

Tom (born 1923)

The death and injury rate of dock workers was very high – exceeded only by that of miners and deep-sea divers. Every docker would have known somebody who had been killed or badly injured at work. Climbing up and down in ships was a cause of serious accidents:

I had a few mates killed. One bloke fell down the hold, sixty foot. The ladder was slippery. As he was going down the ladder he slipped and broke his back. He died, you know.

Jack (born 1924)

If you were turning a case over, it'd catch on a nail or something – I've done quite a few where I'd see the finger off over that.

Tom (born 1923)

The gang would always have a 'whip round' for the family of a colleague who was off work after an accident. Working on barges could also be treacherous:

Sometimes on a canal barge, a long barge, there was a gunnel about that wide [i.e. very narrow] you had to walk along. And this bloke run along and caught his foot in the wrong ring bolt, pitched right in, and the tide was on the way out, running away. Well, I dashed over the barge and as he was going past I grabbed him by his hair and hoiked him out.

Ted (born 1926)

He was reprimanded for this by his boss, who told him he should have thrown him his sleeve to catch hold of, but he said if he had done so, the man 'would have been in Southend by then!'

People who worked on the river came into contact with highly dangerous materials from which there was little, if any protection. Ted described how high-octane gasoline was transported in barges and delivered into petrol stations from the river:

And it was dangerous it was, alright, when they'd empty the barge, they'd open the scuppers up and the fumes in there – if you smoked among the fumes in that it'd go up like a bomb!

Ted (born 1926)

He also worked on the iron boats where chains were used to keep the iron rails together before loading them into ships. This was particularly dangerous in cold weather:

During the winter you had to make sure your chains were all covered up with bags because the links would go 'pop' and you'd have a set of rails coming back at you – you don't know where to run to!

Ted (born 1926)

Rubber was another material which could be lethal. It came in big bales and if one fell out of its net when being loaded or unloaded from a ship's hold it could bounce anywhere:

Well, I know for a fact that my cousin, namesake, Tom, he was in a barge and he was with a feller. One come out of the loophole. It killed him stone dead – bale of rubber. It come from a big height ... yeah but you didn't worry over them things – just got on with the work.

Tom (born 1923)

Sheets of marble were heavy and unwieldy:

There's a bloke got killed ... he was on the marble and a big sheet of marble was laying up on a barge. A tug came along and created a wave that caused the barge to tip, which in turn caused the sheet of marble to fall out on top of the man.

Tom (born 1923)

Some men were willing to put themselves at greater risk in order to earn more money:

> It was bonus they was worried about; the more tonnage they got was bonus – well, you can, by rushing a job, you can always get a lot of accidents.
>
> Ted (born 1926)

People who wanted to earn more chose the more dangerous and difficult commodities to work with because the pay was better:

> I even worked with all the cement mobs ... my back used to be cut to pieces carrying the sugar. I used to carry two hundred weight on your back ... and me hands and all used to be bleeding with cement, but I wanted the money and the money was there.
>
> Jack (born 1924)

The consequences of some hazards only became apparent in later life. Heavy lifting was hard on the spine and must have also caused many hernias. More serious long-term effects on health, including cancer, were caused by exposure to toxic materials such as asbestos. Mined in Russia, it was brought in its raw state on Russian boats to the Port of London and dock workers campaigned long and hard for protective clothing and safer packaging. The dangers were known in the 1950s, but the Government was very slow to act on the information, until eventually the Health and Safety at Work Act was passed in 1974. By this time, large numbers of dockers had been needlessly exposed to asbestos during their working lives. Ted described working with asbestos without any protection at all. This caused him to develop severe lung damage in later life:

> Because we didn't know what it was, we used to make snowballs out of it and chuck it at one another at that time, because the bags was so light, you put twenty bags in the strop, and I used to take nearly four hours to fill a barge up, whereas with other stuff, you know, you could get on with it. We didn't like it because the commodity was so light.
>
> Ted (born 1926)

There were also a lot of deaths and injuries caused by alcohol. Ted qualified as a first-aider in the docks. He told the following gruesome story:

> I was called on a boat, and it was an Indian crew, and it was beer and they'd been pilfering ... and one of them's gone up to get a carton and he got the carton of beer and walked backwards and down the hold he's fallen. Well, he's hit the back of his head ... oh, he was dead because he'd smashed the back of his skull in, you know, cos all the grey matter was at the back ...
>
> Ted (born 1926)

Pay for dockers and stevedores varied according to the type and quantity of work. This was assessed according to the proportion of the ship's capacity being loaded or unloaded:

> We got paid on what we called, 'measurement tonnage'…we used to get paid what we called 'the cubic measurement'.
>
> Jack (born 1924)

A man could earn well if he was prepared to work unsocial hours, like Doris' father:

> Then he went into the docks where the printing place is now.[6] They did twenty four hours on and twenty four hours off. He got £9 a week which was a lot of money in 1923.
>
> Doris (born 1923)

Jack was very happy with his earnings, partly because he would do any kind of work however hard, dangerous or unpleasant:

I always used to have big money in the dock.

Jack (born 1924)

He was even able to start saving, and claimed to have put by what would have been a small fortune at that time:

I joined a bank, Barclay's Bank, in about 1947 and it was a lot of money, a pound then, you know ... I put away about £10,000 in about 3 or 4 years.

Jack (born 1924)

This was not at all typical. Few workers had bank accounts in those days, partly because their earnings were often unreliable. One factor was the weather. Lizzie's father was a docker:

When [there was] bad weather and he couldn't work, he never got paid. See it weren't like it is now – you never got paid if you didn't work. If it rained – well, you were stood off 'til the rain stopped.

Lizzie (born 1927)

Well, the commodities, see, would get wet so you had to cover the hatch up.

Tom (born 1923)

There was, of course, no sick pay or pension for casual workers either. Working times were irregular because the shipping was dependent on times of the tides.

Sometimes I've been to work, started at 8 and finished at 8 the next day to get the ship out – you got to done almost a 24-hour stretch. As I says, the quicker you do the job, the quicker the ship can sail.

Ted (born 1926)

Living nearby, he could 'shoot home' during his breaks and say to his family:

'Well I gotta go back, we're working all night', so then you go back and you'd unload and you finish all the loading and that, and the ship would be on its way rejoicing.

Ted (born 1926)

Jack described his hours of work during the forties:

When we first started it used to be eight o'clock – you called up at quarter to eight of a morning. If you was ten seconds late, two seconds late, you lost your job. Two seconds, one, two, if you wasn't standing there! Then you brought out your card – you went to work on your union card. If you didn't have your union card, you never went to work, so you flashed your union card. Then you went to work, then twelve o'clock you went to dinner, twelve to one. And then you come back, one to three, then you had mobile, what you call 'mobile' – cup of tea, cake, what you wanted, and then you worked 'til seven o'clock.[7] Ten hours a day. Saturdays eight 'til twelve 'til we stopped you know…Sundays was double time ... the pub was open at six o'clock; they'd offer rum and coffee at seven, yeah, pint of Guinness – diesel, you know what I mean, before I went to work.

Jack (born 1924)

It was sometimes frustrating if rain interrupted an easy job. On the other hand, many dockers were not averse to betting on a game of poker in one of the many 'card schools' where they played for money:

When it was a bad job, then we couldn't care less. Before they had the amenity blocks in the dock, well, we used to stand in the ship's alleyway, you know, it might be freezing cold and nowhere to go, but when the amenity blocks came about it was a good idea because you'd go up there and got us playing cards or just biding the time.

Tom (born 1923)

For many years there were no washing facilities for casual workers in the docks:

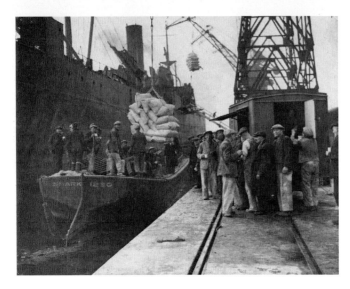

Mobile canteen, 1941. Dockers enjoying 'muggo' – a break from work. (Copyright Museum of Docklands/PLA collection)

You used to go to local baths in Betts Street along the Highway. But I didn't realise they had showers and that, that was exclusively for PLA [Port of London Authority] – they were permanent, they were a permanent man, see. Nothing for the lower people, the ordinary docker.

Tom (born 1923)

The toilet facilities were rudimentary, consisting of a long trough covered with a board with holes cut out of it. The management gave few perks to the workers other than a day off for the King's birthday (and later, the Queen's).

'Perms' – employees of the PLA enjoyed the security of regular work because they were registered with the authority. The PLA employed large numbers of men in the wine vaults and in the carpet and wool warehouses. To obtain a job with the PLA it helped to know someone with influence. Ada's husband had worked in the wine vaults:

My husband worked in St John's [Wharf] 'til the War and then the person who lived next door to me in Riverside spoke for him at the PLA ... You had a regular wage when you worked for the PLA.

Ada (born 1909)

At the height of trading in 1929, the wine vaults in the London Docks, Wapping consisted of a total of twenty-eight miles of maze-like subterranean alleyways, some of which were extended under the water. The royal family, Churchill and other members of the upper classes had cellars there at one time. Working conditions were difficult: the atmosphere was heavy with fumes from rum, whisky, port and other liquors mixed with an oppressive mustiness coming perhaps from the fungus that grew on everything. Even after the Second World War, candles were mainly used to illuminate the vaults.

According to Patrick Hanshaw, they were also infested with rats.[8] It is hardly surprising that some people working in this strange underworld took to drink. Sidney Bell gives an account of working in the wine vaults in Wapping. Hogsheads of port, sherry or rum were rolled along the floor in threes with two men on each side pushing them. They piled them high using ladders known as 'Jacobs'.

The PLA also employed people in a whole variety of jobs in the docks, such as operating the swing bridges. Employees of the PLA were known as 'the blue-eyed boys' because they were favoured by the management.[9] Despite this and the advantages of regular work, Jack and many people like him would rather have starved than work for them:

They done *anything* – no principle! And like, a perm never come out on strike ... Well, we had more strikes and often I used to be out of work for six weeks, two months at a time. Principle! ... that's the way I was brought up.

Jack (born 1924)

Unloading barrels at the wine vaults.
(Copyright Museum of London/
PLA collection)

The PLA also gave a lower rate of pay. Strikes had always been an important part of the history of docking since the great 'docker's tanner strike' of 1889 led by Ben Tillett. During 1911 and 1912 there were prolonged strikes which caused severe hardship amongst the docking families in Wapping. The General Strike was a comparatively short-lived episode, where the dockers came out on strike in sympathy with the miners, from 3-12 May 1926.

'Stoppo' (strikes) was accepted as a way of life amongst dockers. There were many unofficial strikes during which workers received no money from the union and had to manage somehow. Tom refuted the commonly held view that dockers would go on strike for no good reason:

> It was hard work in the dock. You know you get people who didn't know the industry. It was 'All the lazy dockers wanting to go on strike' – you don't go on strike for nothing. 'Lazy dockers' you was called – it was a term to sort of break up the strike, you know.
>
> Tom (born 1923)

People would have to make provision for the hard times during unofficial strikes:

> Like if it went on and on … I had £2 a week put aside for strikes to pay your rent. My Mum used to have it. If you got a house, then you don't have to worry, you know what I mean, if you've shelter.
>
> Jack (born 1924)

Industrial unrest continued after the Second World War – in fact there were thirty-seven strikes in the ten years following VE Day.[10] In 1948-49 there was a dispute over men being suspended for refusing to handle red oxide without protective clothing which gave rise to a state of emergency. The Labour Prime Minister, Clement Atlee, sent the army in to unload the ships. Officially this was reported as successful but the dockers regarded the army as 'poor buffers' who were ineffective at doing the work. Norman and Sal could recall this event dimly, but it clearly did not have much impact on them:

> There wasn't much to that. That was Churchill, [sic] that was, he called the army in.
>
> Norman (born 1919)

> It didn't last long anyway. It didn't bother us, did it, really. The soldiers were there, that's all.
>
> Sal (born 1925)

In 1946 Ernest Bevin[11] introduced the National Dock Labour Scheme with the aim of ending the system of casual working. Although this was not completely successful because the practice of casual

Rum casks in the wine vaults. When the docks were at their busiest there was enough work to employ over 100 coopers to make and maintain the barrels for the wine vaults. (Copyright Tower Hamlets Local History Library)

working continued anyway, it did give dock workers a degree of financial security. According to one ex-docker and union official, this was 'the finest thing that ever happened'.[12]

Tom explained how the National Dock Labour Scheme worked:

> If there was no work all the week, you'd go to the pool which was in Old Gravel Lane as the National Dock Labour Board. Well if you were out of work from Monday see, you used to go there mornings and afternoons where they called [you to] 'bomp on'.
>
> Tom (born 1923)

'Bomping on' meant having the registration book stamped which would entitle the worker to 'fall back pay' if there was no work in the docks. However meagre an amount, this was an improvement on the previous situation:

> The fall back pay in them days when I first started in the dock was £4 8s per week … It was a pittance of course, but, yes, I was married and you had to manage on it.[13]
>
> Tom (born 1924)

An agreement was also made over fixed prices for different commodities. If work was not available at the dock gate, then dockers had the choice of being sent out of Wapping which could be as far as the Tilbury docks, or receiving a minimum daily wage. This was generally unpopular as people far preferred working close to home.

Once they had entered the docks, men were usually obliged to carry on working for as long as they were physically able, because there was no pension to support them in their old age. Fellow workers accommodated their older colleagues wherever they could. Older men of seventy and upwards continued work if only as shed men, opening and shutting doors. As an ex-docker put it:

> We had a lot of little numbers for the old 'uns.
>
> Harry (born around 1923)

Norman's father, who entered the docks late in life after the collapse of his dunnage business (selling second hand rope and timber) was forced to continue working into his old age:

> He must have been about seventy something when he stopped – yeah well, he died when he was eighty three … well, they were very poor in Wapping really, although we weren't too bad off because he always had work, me Dad.
>
> Norman (born 1919)

It was not until 1961 that a pension scheme was finally introduced, thanks to the work of Tim O'Leary, National Secretary of the Transport and General Workers' Union. He himself had attended St Patrick's School in Wapping.

Looking back on their years in the docks, nearly all men would say that they had loved the way of life but would not wish it on their sons. Most men took severance pay when the docks closed in the 1970s and found jobs in the City of London. Some found it hard to adapt, and, like Jack, missed a way of life they could never replace:

> The Thames I love ... I love the river. I think there's nothing like the river. If I'd have won the premium bonds I'd buy one of these flats overlooking the river so I could look out and see the river Thames. I think there's nothing better.
>
> Jack (born 1924)

Although most men were engaged in docking or related work, a minority sought other occupations:

> My father worked in the gasworks ... at the bottom of Malay Street. He was a gas stoker. My father was employed *all* the time. Always in work – he was never called up in the army because he was more important doing the job at the gasworks.
>
> Ernie (born 1913)

During his schooldays in the twenties, Ernie and his sisters always had shoes on their feet, unlike the children from docking families. A regular job was considered a good job.

Mary, who was born in 1912 and moved to Wapping when she was three years old, described her father's work as a foreman horse keeper. He looked after nine or ten horses for his firm, Jacob Alexander and Co., newspaper merchants. The stables were in the ground floor of the house which is still standing at the time of writing:

> And in Mum's bedroom there used to be a loophole where Dad used to go through early of a morning and cut all the chaff ready for the carmen to feed [the horses] ...[14] He used to have big bales of hay up in the loft. I think he had some type of machine there. And to save going down and opening up very early of a morning, he used to go through there, cut all the hay and then he used to come back and have his breakfast before he went down and opened up ... and he had a gas copper down there which he used to keep just to boil water up for washing the horses.
>
> Mary (born 1912)

Many men, and their fathers before them, had worked in local boot and shoe manufacturers, or in the big local breweries such as Trumans and Charringtons. Some worked for smaller firms, and many young men joined the army as professional soldiers. Kathleen's father had worked for the council:

> Me Dad started in the Corporation of London when he was fourteen and finished when he was sixty – he only had one job all his life.
>
> Kathleen (born 1934)

His job was sweeping up rubbish on Tower Bridge. As he disliked having to clear away the dead pigeons he devised an easy way of dealing with them: he brushed them onto the road so they would get flattened before sweeping them down the drain. All jobs have their methodology!

When he was working as a wood machinist, Norman had an altercation with his boss:

> Mr Cook's was on the corner of Old Gravel Lane and The Highway ... Yeah well, this chap was getting a ha' penny more than me, and he was a sander and I was a machinist. I'd done everything, know what I mean.
>
> Norman (born 1919)

He went to ask the manager for a pay rise, who refused, so he left in a huff and found work elsewhere. He returned a few days later to give in his notice:

Know what happened? They got together the manager – they got the governor and foreman down in the shop together, took me in the office, asked me 'why?' and I told them, and they said: 'We'll offer you another nine pence!' Another *nine pence!* so I said 'No, you're too late' and they was choked, and they said, 'If you ever want your job back you can come'. I said. 'No, I don't think so'. But see, they take liberties don't they, sometimes.

Norman (born 1919)

Bill made his boyhood dreams come true:

First job was in a small leather factory up by the Troxy.[15] Just an ordinary little thing, you know, but it was right by the railway, and during quiet periods I could go to the top floor and stand by the window where the railway was, and I was only about eight or ten foot from the line, and I could see all these lovely big engines coming along there, and I thought 'that's a better, more romantic job. I think I'll have a bit of that.'

Bill (born 1926)

So, without any qualifications or formal training, he became a fireman in a locomotive:

We were all supposed to start off as cleaners, but during the wartime, they were so hard up for people, they never cleaned anything, you know. They used to show a little bit of it – they had little bits of machinery with bits cut off so you could see the inner workings of it … and that was it! – start the fireman's job, so I used to think, well it's a bit hard on some of the drivers – you had this green boy come with him thrown in at the deep end sort of thing and make steam in the thing all day long – but we got by alright.

Bill (born 1926)

Some people who ran small businesses or were self-employed were comparatively well off. Everyone, however, was affected by the Depression in the 1930s:

My father's business collapsed, you know, in the period just before the Second World War because, of course, nobody was buying houses because they were afraid they were going to be bombed. So he went through a very bad patch with his business and then it had to be wound up.

Audrey (born 1927)

Luckily her mother, a teacher, was able to take over as the breadwinner. For most women, this sort of flexibility and earning power was not easily available, and many families had a struggle to survive.

Notes

1. In his autobiographical account of a docking family in Wapping, *Nothing is Forever*, Patrick Hanshaw writes that his father had witnessed fights at the dock gate when he was working in the thirties. The notorious casual work system was reformed after the Second World War.
2. The origin of the phrase 'piping for work' is not clear – Patrick Hanshaw in his autobiography, *Nothing is Forever*, surmises that it is an Irish expression referring to the pecking order of pipers in an Irish band.
3. West India Dock.
4. Sidney Bell who was born in 1906 in Wapping, source Museum in Docklands transcript.
5. Source: *The City and East London Observer* 18 March 1939.
6. *News International*
7. Twenty-seven 'mobile kitchens' were actually kept at fixed sites.
8. *Nothing is Forever*, Patrick Hanshaw, description of wine vaults.
9. According to Jack Banfield., born 1907 (source Museum in Docklands transcript 1985).
10 Alan Palmer, *The East End*.
11. At that time Foreign Secretary in the Labour Government, formerly war-time Minister of Labour and originally a docker himself.
12. Personal communication from Maurice Foley, ex-union official.
13. He is referring to about the time when the Dock Labour Scheme was introduced i.e. 1946/47.
14. Driver of horse and cart.
15. The Troxy Cinema.

5

MAKING ENDS MEET

We were one of the richest countries in the world!

Jack (born 1924)

All the money, where did it come from? Where was it then? And we had the *Empire*, didn't we!

Doris (born 1923)

Despite their proximity to the wealth of trade from the docks, just getting by from day to day was a struggle for most ordinary families. The main priority was to feed all the family:

We always had a dinner – I don't know really how she done it, you know – but my Dad used to give her – he used to earn £4 10s per week, my father. I'm going back to 1931.

Janet (born 1921)

My mother had £2 5s a week and she kept us all on that, but we all had a good dinner.

Lilly (born 1925)

When his father could not get work in the docks, Norman's mother was obliged to step in:

When I was young she used to work. Like every mother had to sub – especially them days they had to work to get a little bit of money.

Norman (born 1919)

People describe living from hand to mouth, with just enough money to pay for the barest necessities:

Thursday, we've got no money have we! We just got paid weekly.

Doris (born 1923)

Money was scarce, weren't it – ay, you'd be broke Wednesday, but as long as you had a penny – a penny in your gas 'ould last a day, because you had a coal fire, but you had gas for your cooking and your light. You'd put a penny in your gas and it would last you best part of a day.

Lizzie (born 1927)

Even lighting the fire, they used to save the orange peel, potato peel, dry [it] and they'd start the fire up. They wasn't mean – it was survival.

Ron (born 1921)

Meals had to be carefully planned:

Up Watney Street, you'd get half a dozen eggs and they'd have to last.

Janet (born 1921)

We used to walk over to Southwark Park because it was free – open air – didn't have the three ha'pence fare so we'd walk from the New Park.

Doris (born 1923)

It was cheaper for people to make their own clothes if they had the skills:

One of my sisters was a qualified dressmaker – she used to get a remnant for say, three shillings, and make me something.

Lizzie (born 1927)

Most children had to make do with hand-me-downs from their siblings. Ernie however, counted himself lucky in this respect:

I had seven sisters so they couldn't hand down any clothes and that. If they bought me anything it had to be new!

Ernie (born 1913)

The poorest people bought all their clothing second hand. Janet recalled that her father mended her boots and shoes over and over again:

He'd do it in the time he had, but otherwise it was up the road to get 'em done – soled and heeled, don't matter what the top looked like as long as it was soled and heeled.

Janet (born 1921)

My Dad used to mend our boys' boots himself. He used to buy the leather and bang it on and cut all round … 'there you are! another pair, what's the next pair?' he used to say. But that's the way you survived, because you had to mend your own shoes and boots, so we used to say 'Can we have two studs on there?' and he'd say 'Well, what d'you want them for?' – We'd dance all up the Orchard, and he'd bang a couple more in, and he

Haberdashers, Watney Street. C. Shelstone, hosier, draper and outfitter was in Watney Street from 1919-38. (Copyright Tower Hamlets Local History Library)

said, 'Will you shut that racket out!' We'd be tap dancing away! We had the cheek to come out of the pictures and we'd all pretend we were film stars and we were dancing stars and God knows what!

Grace (born 1921)

When Lilly got a scholarship to a good secondary school not more than 1½ miles away from home, the cost of the bus fares made a serious hole in the family budget:

See, I mean, my mother could ill afford to even send me to St Bernard's. She had to buy me the uniform – so you can imagine. And we had to pay our fare, living in Matilda House, so we had to get the bus up Dock Street, get another one right along up to Commercial Road.

Lilly (born 1925)

Tom's mother, like many other mothers, was in charge of money. His father left his wages out for her on the mantelpiece when he came home:

Mother was, I'd say, she was a good manager, you know. Cos me father in them days, he used to get paid every night.

Tom (born 1923)

Groups of friends or work colleagues clubbed together to share goods they would not otherwise have been able to afford. Ethel remembered paying 1s a week so that she could take it in turns to wear new clothes or a new handbag, with twelve other women:

You had to pick a number and whoever picked the [right] number had the handbag or underslips you know, vests and that.

Ethel (born 1916)

Some people hired their clothes out:

My eldest sister used to let clothes out for so much a week, and I'd take some to work with me if any of the girls wanted anything, and I'd collect the money Friday.

Mary (born 1912)

Lizzie's family belonged to a Christmas savings club:

The women used to put a shilling each away, and the men used to put a shilling, and then we'd all be together Christmas, and that used to pay for all our food, all our drink and a little present on the tree for all the children.

Lizzie (born 1927)

No matter how thrifty people tried to be, many resorted to buying on credit or 'on tick' from local shopkeepers. Door-to-door salesmen or 'tally men' took advantage of the situation, selling inferior goods at inflated prices. They tended to visit when the husband was out, leaving goods without demanding repayment at first, to make it more tempting. Some women were driven into the clutches of private money lenders since goods could be seized back by the tallyman if payment was not forthcoming. The clergy of St Peter's Church tried to provide an alternative to the tallymen by selling clothing at low cost. Lilly remembered that the tallyman was always coming round to sell a wide range of household goods when she was growing up in the thirties. One of the women in her tenement building had a radiogram which she had bought:

… on tally – everything was on tick. On a Friday night we used to have a man come round. He was always called 'taché man', because he came round with an attaché case! And he used to sell little bits of clothing, bag of tea, and you'd pay him on tick. Coal man, same thing, used to come round on a Sunday morning to collect his money for the coal.

Lilly (born 1927)

In Ethel's street of small houses all huddled together, there was pressure to keep up with the Jones's. Ethel recalls they all had 'lovely white lace curtains. They all had them on tick—so much a week.'

Many people relied heavily on the pawn shop to keep afloat. Everyone knew Percy Hyde's which was just outside Wapping.¹ Peggy could describe the premises in detail:

> You took clothes and boots there and washing – you pawned your washing, but the other front part, that's where you took jewellery, clocks, umbrellas and things like that. And perhaps they'd have musical instruments. And when you wanna get the things out of pawn, you give them the ticket and you paid a little bit extra on 'em for having it. They must have done alright from it, and some people never got their parcels out, and after a time they sold all that stuff.
>
> Peggy (born 1920)

People were quite secretive about using the pawn shop (referred to euphemistically as 'uncle' or 'bullock's horn'.) Wapping people preferred to pay someone else to take their belongings there, so that nobody would know about it:

> There used to be a woman, I think her name was Mrs Green, she'd have a big pram and she used to take bundles up to the pawn shop.
>
> Janet (born 1921)

The price for this discretion was a few coppers. Janet went on to say however, that her family stopped asking Mrs Green to go for them when they suspected she had been gossiping. Using the pawnshop was better than borrowing money from other people:

> My mother had money – I wouldn't go and ask my mother. My mother used to say to me 'Buy a bit of gold, son. If you've got gold, you've got money. Go down to the pawn shop, no-one knows your business.' So I used to buy gold, so I've got rings in there – gold rings – big lovers' knot, great bit thick lovers' knot, *that* thick – never wear them – and they used to go in the pawn. When on holiday, I'd say 'I'll pawn me rings' and when I was on strike, for money, and when I went to work I'm out of pawn again. *But I didn't ask from nobody.*
>
> Jack (born 1924)

For many people, using the pawn shop was part of their weekly routine:

> I mean sometimes the rent wasn't paid, and there was ructions then. Someone's best suit used to go in on Monday and come out Saturday, to go back again.
>
> Janet (born 1921)

You could pawn virtually anything. Dockers were even known to pawn their hooks. Some surprising items found their way to the pawnshop:

> The PLA, the dock police, they gave a party for the kids every Christmas and they gave 'em boots. Well, they found out that some of the boots was being sent to the pawn shop, so then, what they done, they branded them 'PLA' so the pawn broker looked at them and they obviously instructed them – cos the kids wasn't benefiting by them …
>
> Ron (born 1921)

Some of the worst times were during strikes in the docks. During Ernie's childhood in the twenties, there were still many children growing up in abject poverty:

> I went to school at St Peter's School, and I can assure you that there were more kids without shoes on than with shoes.
>
> Ernie (born 1913)

When unemployment was high during the thirties, there were still some children who did not have shoes. Annie, who grew up in a comfortable home during that period, recorded some impressions of the poverty surrounding her:

St Peter's London Docks boys' school, Red Lion Street, *c.* 1915. Several boys look undernourished and are barefoot.

Only a few years ago my sister told me of the time she called on her friend to go to school, only to find that she could not go as she had no shoes to wear. My sister promptly returned home, took a pair of mine and gave them to her – an act which, to my sister's relief was never discovered. This was life in Wapping just prior to the war.

Annie (born 1925)

Unemployment could lead to destitution:

There was a lady and a man who lived four doors away from us. He couldn't get a job anywhere and they threw him out and they went to live under the arches.

Annie (born 1925)

Because her family was much better off than most, Annie's mother always made a Christmas meal for the neighbours' children. Otherwise they would not have enjoyed any celebration at all:

One year, when Mum gave that party, I went out into the kitchen and the remains of our turkey was on the kitchen table with a cloth over it, you see, and there was this wee boy eating it all up, stuffing it all into his face [miming frantic eating] – you know, getting it all in so nobody could see him.

Annie (born 1925)

Lilly, who came from the poorest of families, had this to say about her childhood Christmases:

Christmas came and went. You never had nothing – no, never see a Christmas cracker, lucky if you saw an apple or an orange and as for a turkey – that was in your imagination!

Lilly (born 1925)

In Ellen Kemp's family, the children went hungry because their father spent all his money in the pub. In her autobiography *Don't let them see you cry,* she describes a typical family meal:

Everyday, Mum would buy one big cottage loaf which had to last to the next day. This was Harry's job at tea time; he would cut off one thick slice for each of us watched closely by us so that no one got a thicker slice.

Ellen Kemp (born c. 1928)

The appalling scale of the malnutrition amongst young working-class men was brought to light during conscription for the Second World War. Many of these youths enjoyed regular meals and adequate clothing for the first time in their lives when they joined the army:

> I never slept in no pyjamas, I didn't know what pyjamas was! I mean where I went to school it used to be 'Stand up all the boys whose fathers died in the War', and it was 'Stand up all the boys whose fathers was in prison' and in the corner there'd be all old gear – coats, you'd put an old coat on, it'd be all long, all down your ankles, you know what I mean – a pair of trousers or waistcoat – and you'd take 'em home and your Mum would alter them.

Jack (born 1924)

When his father died from his war wounds his mother received a very small widow's pension, without which, he said, they would have starved.

Lilly's mother had also had a war widow's pension from the First World War but it was stopped when she and her siblings were born, because they were illegitimate.

Illness in the breadwinner could be disastrous for the family finances. Nevertheless people went to enormous lengths to be self reliant so as to avoid the stigma of charity, or even worse, state intervention. The first port of call in times of dire need was the extended family. Doris' father lost his job because of a chronic illness:

> But we didn't go without because we had aunts and uncles round the area, men working that looked after us.

Doris (born 1923)

Lloyd George's National Health Insurance Act of 1911 allowed working men sickness benefit of 10s per week, provided they could supply a doctor's certificate, but this was nowhere near enough to feed a family. Ron's family just about coped:

> Well, you just carried on, they just eked out, as children, they would send you round to your Granny, perhaps you would get food, and they had to get together like, and plus, I must say, obviously some of them survived with gear that come out of the docks. If it wasn't the docks it might have been on the horse and carts, where the carman was transporting stuff, and he had a bit of cheese, or he had some tea – take it round to so and so.

Ron (born 1921)

Mary, whose family was better off than most of the neighbours, remembered how her parents helped people out:

> Dad always went and bought the meat and you'd think he was feeding the five thousand! Sometimes he used to buy an H bone of beef and none of them would eat it the next day, and there was a family round the corner, poor woman, her husband was in bleeding bed, and she had a lot of children and Mum used to do it all up and take it round to her.

Mary (born 1912)

Mary's parents also held Christmas parties for their neighbours' children:

> Christmas time we'd have a big Christmas tree up here – reach the ceiling, and it'd be packed with everything you could think of, and they'd have boys names in one hat, and girls in the other, so girls wouldn't get a boy's toy, and the boys wouldn't get a girl's toy.

Mary (born 1912)

Organised charity had been established in Wapping for many years. During the dock strikes of 1911 and 1912 there had been various coffee shops where dockers' families could have free bread and jam, soup, cocoa or tea at different times of the day. All three churches were very active in providing charity for the poor and destitute. Benn's Chapel had also been an important support to the poor, since its inception in the mid-nineteenth century. Elsie, whose father had a secure job in the local gasworks, remembers going in there as a child in the twenties:

> There used to be a chapel, corner of Greenbank, called 'Benn's Chapel' and they took all the kids whose father was out of work in to have tea. Course I'd put me face in – somebody said "Ere, your Dad's not out of work, you're not on strike!' I said, 'no, but he's on his holidays!' and they let me stop!'
>
> Elsie (born 1913)

Ellen Kemp writes that her older sister took her to St Patrick's school when she was only two years old. There, she was given free dinners and supervised, because her parents were unable either to feed or look after her. Children as malnourished as Ellen qualified for free hot milk which was introduced for the most needy in some schools in 1934.

It is not difficult to understand why most people regarded state welfare as absolutely the last resort. The system in place before the Second World War was harsh and humiliating in the extreme, and people were absolutely terrified of being sent to the workhouse. This fear persisted long after the workhouses were closed in 1929:

> I can remember when the recession was on in the thirties, there was me brother out of work, two of me sisters out of work. You never got what like you get now, 'social'.
>
> Lizzie (born 1927)

> They used to call it, 'R.O.' You got a voucher to spend up Sainsbury's. They wouldn't give you money, they'd give vouchers to go and shop and buy food.'
>
> Nellie (born 1916)

> I remember as a kid, butchers shops would have tickets up in the winder called R.O. tickets – well it wouldn't say 'R.O', pardon me, it would be 'relief tickets taken here' that allowed people who was on low income, what we classify now, they would get a grant of going into a butcher's shop and getting the meat at a reduced rate … but family life around here wouldn't allow you to do that because it was a stigma – you was at the bottom of the league.
>
> Ron (born 1921)

> I can remember when my Dad was in the docks, if he didn't go to work for the whole week he'd get nothing. We'd have to get a food ticket and then we'd go up and get our groceries from the shop.
>
> Sal (born 1925)

In a small community like Wapping, it was obvious who was on benefit:

> They had to queue at that arch because the Relieving Officer was where The Lodge is now.[2] My father hated it, because he was a very, sort of, proud man – I suppose I am. Never take charity.
>
> Doris (born 1923)

People bitterly resented the means testing visit from the relieving officer who took all earnings coming into the household, including that of children, into account. If a young person living with his or her parents received a pay rise, the father's benefit would be reduced accordingly, even if he was still unemployed. Children above the school-leaving age of fourteen could be forced to go out to work:

> Before my Mum could get something, my two sisters, they had to go cleaning over the Infirmary … and if he thought you owned something that was valuable, he'd say 'Sell it for money'.
>
> Lizzie (born 1927)

If you had *anythink* they made you sell it! You sold your table or chairs to get money – it was terrible, and it was only because there was thieves and people like that, where my mother used to get the stuff from … I don't know what would have happened!

Jack (born 1924)

Doris recalled how angry she had felt when the Unemployment Assistance Board turned her down:

It was a man with pince-nez glasses. 'Have you worked this week?' So I said 'Yes up 'til …', 'Well you go back and get your money!' We didn't get a thing! I mean when I think of men standing up on Pennington Street in the freezing cold.[3]

Doris (born 1923)

If a person had a chronic illness which made them unfit for work, there was no safety net. Beggars were part of the community:

We used to have another man used to come round Wapping Sunday morning, playing the penny whistle, and he used to have a thing on him that he suffered from epileptic fits, and he had a wife and about five children and people used to throw money out to him.

Lizzie (born 1927)

The association between the hospital and the workhouse partly explains the fear people had of being sent into hospital, which indeed can still be encountered amongst some elderly people at the time of writing. Pam, who was working as a 'Lady Almoner' in St George's in the East Hospital in 1956, was surprised when one of her clients, a very independent-spirited woman, insisted on going to a home which had previously been a workhouse. When she went to visit her in her new home at Southern Grove Lodge, the inside was virtually unchanged since its days as a workhouse. Pam remembered:

Their room where they sat all day was one large room covered with lino, and there were trestle tables down it with hard chairs around, and that's where they sat all day – wards virtually. There were iron beds with a tiny locker next to it where they could bring, as you can in a hospital, a few possessions like that, and that was their long-term home, so you can imagine, it was an entirely grisly place.

Once installed, the client, a forceful lady with a silver-topped stick, realised she had made a terrible mistake. She became very disturbed, and took to drink.

Before the Second World War, few ordinary people had any possibility of saving money for the long term. George, the son of a successful businessman, remembered how his father was held in awe because he had a bank account and could use a cheque book. Although many people did enjoy a better lifestyle after the Second World War, it was not always easy for them to adjust. People could not change their thrifty ways just like that:

I think it wasn't really 'til we moved over here, that was in about 1968, I can remember I could start saving up a few bob. And it's always made me careful with money, cos my daughter, she's always nagging me 'Mum, buy a new three piece!' I says 'Cost over £1,000, what do I want to spend £1,000 at my time of life for? If I've got it, leave it, yous have it and enjoy it, I won't enjoy it!' See that's how it makes you.

Lilly (born 1925)

Notes

1. In Cannon Street Road.
2. A block of flats for elderly people at the time of writing.
3. Men waiting on the cobbles for work in the docks.

6

FOOD

The subject of family meals reawakened many happy memories. People could picture their mother or grandmother in the scullery minding the stew, which would be bubbling away for hours:

> My mother used to get scrag end of lamb, put that in the pot and simmer it away and chuck everything in it that she could think of, you know.
>
> Grace (born 1921)

> She was always cooking, my grandmother ... Nanny used to do lovely boiled beef, salt beef, carrots, pease pudding – she used to do it in a rag and drop it in the pot while the cabbage and everything else was cooking – she used to do it all in the same pot.
>
> Angie (Ethel's daughter)

Ernie was very enthusiastic about his mother's 'beautiful' cooking. He added:

> All my sisters' young men, they're all dead now, but they would remember her cooking. I think that's why they used to court my sisters – for the stew!
>
> Ernie (born 1913)

> We used to buy the ox tails, and believe me, you've never tasted [anything like it] in all your life – it falls off the bone ... but it takes about three hours to cook.
>
> Ethel (born 1916)

Most people enjoyed simple home cooking. Women chose the cheapest cuts of meat, such as the scrag of lamb to make into suet puddings, meat pies and stews. Ada's father did some of the cooking:

> Me Dad used to fry a piece of meat, you know, stewing beef and that, and then he used to put these sheeps' tails or any little tails of whatever meat he used, and then we used to have another nice big stew because that could go on the stove itself and simmer and simmer.
>
> Ada (born 1909)

People usually bought a 'penn'orth of pot herbs' – a selection of vegetables such as an onion, a turnip and a carrot to go with the stew with potatoes. Kathleen remembered visiting her grandmother as a child and asking to go and see the rabbits in the yard. Her grandmother said:

> I've made you a lovely stew. We all decided to go and see the rabbits and of course the rabbits wasn't there!
>
> Kathleen (born 1934)

There was also a man who went round Wapping on his horse and cart, selling rabbits in a basket. He charged extra to skin them and cut off their heads, ready for the pot:

> Once a week, yeah, used to get rabbit. I loved rabbit, rabbit stew, threw it in the oven, the rabbit with slices

of belly of pork – aw it was lovely!

Nellie (born 1916)

Lizzie, who came from a large family, described how her thrifty mother managed to make enough food to go round:

> It was a lot of bones and all, and would go in a big pot and the butcher would *give* you a bit of suet (you never bought the suet like now) and your mother'd put that in a big pot with the pot herbs, and my Mum would always buy an Edward's cube, that was a big thing but like the Oxos are, and that'd go in, and she'd make dumplings and went and bought like the potatoes [for] when you come home from school, dinner time. Mind you, you had more veg and gravy than meat, you only had a little bit of meat.

Lizzie (born 1927)

Suet dumplings and puddings – both savoury and sweet – were staple foods. Puddings could either be made in a dish or tied up in a piece of cloth and boiled:

> I used to make a steak and kidney pudding, get a basin, make the pudding and put the top on, you know, the pastry, like the flour and that, and put it right down the basin, so when they had their dinner that used to be dry, so they used to have jam on their pudding.

Nellie (born 1916)

> I used to save my dumpling. Although it'd been cooked in the gravy it'd go on a little plate or a saucer and I used to have sugar on my dumplings.

Lizzie (born 1927)

Home cooking had to be filling:

> And my Mum used to make a meat pie of corned beef, like cos you could get corned beef, and she'd make pastry and she'd put this corned beef between it, and you'd have corned beef, but you did get [fed], we weren't hungry really.

Nellie (born 1916)

Apart from the pot herbs and potatoes, people did not eat many vegetables. They might have bubble and squeak made from leftovers, or pease pudding wrapped up in a piece of cloth and dropped in the pot. People did not eat fruit regularly either, and salad was for Sundays or special occasions. Every now and again mothers might make a cake such as a rock cake or coconut cake, especially if there were visitors. Popular 'afters' were rice pudding and bread pudding – another dish made from leftovers, using bread soaked in milk, mixed with egg and boiled in a piece of cloth.

Both Catholics and Protestants ate fish on Fridays, and of course, people loved their eels which many people bought live and used to jelly themselves at home. They always carried on wriggling after they had been killed. Some people were convinced that food tasted better when they were young:

> They used to be lovely potatoes, the lovely King Edwards but you don't see them now do you? We used to have them with all the dirt on them, you know, but they used to be lovely with bacon.

Ada (born 1909)

> When you had chicken you could smell it down the street, not like a chicken now, you can't even smell the chicken in the oven!'

Ernie (born 1913)

Perhaps one reason for this was because the food was fresh, unprocessed and free of chemicals.

Until the late 1920s, many families did not have an oven, and did their cooking on the open fire:

> Course my mother had a stove without oven didn't she, years ago, the fire oven – an oven next to the fire.

Ada (born 1909)

When you had your fire you wouldn't waste it if you could cook in your oven, and you always had a kettle on the boil on the fire, everybody, you had like a little thing, [a trivet] what you push round, and you always had the kettle on there boiling. Anybody come, you made 'em a cup of tea.

Lizzie (born 1927)

Other people did their cooking on kitchen ranges. When the older houses and tenements were knocked down, the flats which replaced them were connected to the gas supply. Even then, many people still did not have ovens, so they had to cook on the stove, or boil food in the copper. In the twenties and thirties, if they fancied a roast dinner on a Sunday, people without ovens could pay the baker to cook a joint of meat for them. The dripping from the meat kept the family going during the week:

On the main Sunday dinner, if it was lamb or H bone of beef, me mother used to put suet on top, and cook the potatoes, and when it was finished, the fat would be put in a basin, and when it was cooled right off, it was dripping, and our main thing was of a tea time, or [if] you come in hungry, the Neville's loaf, the lumpy bit, that'd be broke off, cut in the middle and she'd put some dripping in it and some salt and out you'd go again.

Ted (born 1926)

Ted remembered the dripping with real relish:

Well it was marvellous because if you tipped it up they used to get all the jelly and all the meat – you used to scrape all that on-it was the best part!

Ted (born 1926

Those who were better off, such as Mary's family, used to have three proper meals a day, including a hot dinner and an evening meal with meat. In poorer families bread and jam or bread and dripping was a substitute for a meal if there was nothing else going:

Don't remember having breakfast – no-bit of bread and jam, I expect.

Elsie (born 1913)

Lilly, who came from a very poor home, actually had to go out and earn her evening meal after coming home from school:

When we came home in the evening you could have a cup of tea. There'd probably be bread and jam or something like that, and if you wanted anything in the evening you had to do errands for somebody before you could go round the fish shop and get a penn'orth of chips.

Lilly (born 1925)

At that time you could buy a piece of fish for 2d or a portion of chips for 1d. Often this was all Dolly and her mother could afford:

She worked hard, she worked very hard. I can picture her now, 'Well, don't know what we're gonna have for tea – haven't got any money' … I had to go and get a penn'orth of chips and they used to sort out the cracklings'.

Dolly (born 1912)

The bits of fried batter that had fallen off the fish were known as the 'cracklings'.

Food portions had to be carefully controlled in some large families so that everybody got their share:

When you were kids you never had a whole bit of fish 'til you left school; you'd have half a piece of fish – and like – it didn't hurt us. Like you never had an 'ole apple, an 'ole orange; your mother would cut it all up in quarters.

Lizzie (born 1927)

Ron admitted that there were times when it was difficult to put together a meal:

> Even if they made you a lettuce sandwich there was always something to eat and I sit down now and say 'how did they ever manage?'
>
> Ron (born 1921)

There must have been times when people did not manage during the twenties and thirties, especially during the dockers' strikes or when the father of the family could not get work. Yet nobody could remember going hungry. Lilly was emphatic on this point:

> NEVER, NEVER, NEVER, NEVER! We were very poverty-stricken but we *never* went hungry and we always had food.
>
> Lilly (born 1925)

Dolly, whose mother earned her living as a sack repairer, also said that she had always had enough to eat:

> No I wasn't hungry – there was certain things you would have liked to have had, but me mother just couldn't buy 'em, just never had the money, poor thing – worked hard to look after us – couldn't have luxuries. You was lucky to get what you did get.
>
> Dolly (born 1912)

Although children may have had enough food to fill their bellies, clearly very many were not growing up on a healthy, balanced diet. Perhaps it was because there was not much to eat that people really appreciated what they had. Ernie seemed to think this was the case:

> You enjoyed your food more because you were hungrier than what you are today. There was many a time we only had bread and jam for tea but we really enjoyed it just the same, we never used to feel hungry.
>
> Ernie (born 1913)

In many families, the father got the best food:

> Sometimes, he used to – where we'd have a stew or something, he'd have a bit of steak or pork chop, but he used always to like his steak or beef raw – underdone ... but in the week it had to be pork chop with a kidney for him, or a bit of rump steak or something. We'd have whatever was going – the scrag end!
>
> Janet (born 1921)

> When we had shrimps for tea and winkles and whatever, she used to pick 'em all for me Dad – not so much for us!
>
> Norman (born 1919)

Most families tried to manage to have a special meal on Sundays. Whilst many a child skipped breakfast or just had toast or porridge, some could look forward to the luxury of an egg on Sunday or even bacon or salt fish too. Even if they could not afford to eat meat during the week, most families would have some kind of roast joint such as an 'H' bone of beef for their Sunday dinner. For Sunday tea, the tradition in Wapping was watercress or celery with cockles and winkles and herrings from the Jews' market. In the winter they toasted muffins on the fire.

Shopping was a time-consuming part of a mother's daily routine. Local butchers sold cheap cuts including boiled sheep's head, and offal in the form of brains and tripe. There was also a variety of cooked meats such as calves' foot jelly. Ada's father went to the tripe dresser in Algate:

> He used to sell this bullock's cheek and tripe. Of course, we never used to have it, but sometimes we had the tripe, but my Dad used to buy this bullock's cheek in a piece.
>
> Ada (born 1909)

You know, you done your shopping everyday because you never had no fridges and that.

Lizzie (born 1927)

We had no fridges in those days, we had a box and just a wire mesh in the front in the summertime. That was your fridge years ago.

Tom (born 1923)

People used to have cupboards in the yard to keep meat and that in – you never let anything go bad!

Mary (born 1912)

Many women chose to do the bulk of their shopping in Watney Market rather than in the local shops in Wapping because there they could find real bargains, such as at the meat auction on Sundays. Women generally walked about three-quarters of a mile there and back, often with one or two daughters to help carry the shopping home:

I mean, when I was first married [in the early 1930s] you could go and get a leg of lamb for half a crown and that would last you all the week if you wasn't big meat eaters. [2]

Mary (born 1912)

Watney Market was a very lively place with a lot of choice and competition between the different stall holders:

That was a market with all the costermongers, and it was a variety [show] on its own, you know! The cockney people were very witty. But it was the variety of life, you know, the spice of life and all.

Tom (born 1923)

Spanning two main roads, in its heyday Watney Market had nearly 100 stalls selling a wide range of food and clothes. [3] In the thirties, there was a good choice of fresh fish including live eels, and several butchers to choose from with the sides of meat hanging outside in rows. There was also a stall selling cats' meat. You could find everything you could possibly want there, from second-hand clothing and hats to perfumed soaps made from 'brown oil'. The sweet stall displayed delicious home-made toffee and confectionery. The market stayed open until as late as 9 p.m. and was also open on Sundays:

And at Christmas time they [the fruit stall holders] would start stopping out all night. They used to do all their stall up and have the big braziers at the side to keep warm all night. It was lovely, the fruit was lovely. Better than what you can buy now.

Peggy (born 1920)

Ted remembered queuing up in Sainsbury's, which was established in Watney Market before the Second World War:

My Dad loved salt butter, and on the counter, I always remember as a boy, they had it in big blocks and he'd cut a chunk off, and he'd have a board and he'd pat it together, then make a square, and put it on the scales.

Ted (born 1926)

After a big shopping trip, people liked to have a sit down. Most likely they would end up at the pie and mash shop, where they could select live eels to be cooked to order.

Wapping people also shopped at the Jews' Market, just a short walk away. [4] Like other East Enders, they had developed a taste for Jewish foods such as pickled herrings, pickled cucumbers, Jewish bread and bagels.

Shopping took a long time, since there was no such thing as pre-packaging:

In them days you used to have a big lump of bacon; you'd cut slices off like that and smack it in a bit of paper and weigh it up.

Grace (born 1921)

Butcher's stall, Watney Market, 1910. The stall was owned by the Waller family. (Copyright Tower Hamlets Local History Library)

Cooking salt had to be sawn off the block and people bought small quantities of loose tea in little packs for a few pence. Instead of buying jam in jars, one could take a cup from home, which first of all was weighed, then filled with jam, and then the weight of the cup was subtracted from the total weight with the jam.

Until the Second World War there was a great variety of street traders who came into Wapping. Each trader had his own day. People remembered the melancholy call of the rag-and-bone man, who gave children a cup or a goldfish (which always died) in exchange for rags. Other street traders sold off fresh food in season at knock-down prices:

> And when there was a glut of tomatoes and radishes and strawberries they'd call out. You'd come down and buy.
>
> Lizzie (born 1927)

> There used to be the fish man that came round. His name was Dan. He used to sell greengroceries on the week and fish on Friday and seafoods on Sunday.
>
> Sal (born 1925)

'Dan, the winkle man' did a roaring trade in shrimps, cockles, winkles and whelks from his barrow on Sundays. Watercress went well with seafood:

> Old Mr Tuck on a Sunday, he used to stand up in Greenbank and he'd have a box in front of him – watercress, a ha'penny a bundle, and we used to buy them bundles for Sunday tea.
>
> Ted (born 1926)

Sunday was also the muffin man's day:

> The old muffin man used to come round with a basket on his head and he'd ring a bell.
>
> Norman (born 1919)

A man rode into Wapping on a tricycle selling pies from a big box. Then there was also the milkman. Although many people preferred condensed milk in tins because it kept longer, they could also buy their milk every day from the milkman:

> The milkman used to come around on his horse and cart with a great big urn ... and you'd go down with your jug and he'd get you whatever milk you wanted and he'd come round every day ... he was in the dairy at the back, and that shop, if people were hard up he'd let you put food on tick.
>
> Lizzie (born 1927)

Some people, especially those who could not get to the market, relied on vegetables being delivered to their door. If they were not at home when the salesman came to deliver, he left the goods and they paid him the next time they saw him. Sal remembered the 'cats' meat man', who went from door to door with a basket full of what was probably horse meat on skewers. If there was nobody in, he just threw the meat up the passage.

One of the best treats for a child was home-made Italian ice cream, sold from a barrow.[5] You could either buy a penny or ha'penny wafer, or ask him to fill a basin from home:

> And then in the winter he sold chestnuts and hot − it was like Ribena, but they used to call it blackcurrant. You could buy it hot for about a ha'penny or a penny.
>
> Lizzie (born 1927)

Lizzie described how shopping, recycling and entertainment were all rolled into one:

> We used to have a horse and cart, and it had a roundabout on it. Most people bought a penn'orth jam and mustard pickle. You never had a jam jar, you went round there to the barrel and he give you a penn'orth of jam in the cup, and he used to come round with this barrel. If you had a jam jar, you got a penny back if you took it, if you bought your beer in a beer bottle with screws, you got tuppence on your beer bottle, but we'd take it [the money] for a ride And the kids who couldn't go on it, who didn't have [any money] to pay, they all give it a push and you'd sit on this roundabout and it'd go round and round ...
>
> Lizzie (born 1927)

By today's standards food was not plentiful and the diet somewhat monotonous. Any variety was seasonal. Foreign cuisine at that time had not reached the British working class and many people in Wapping could not afford to eat properly. Despite all this, they apparently did not feel deprived. Far from it:

> In Old Gravel Lane there used to be a fish shop. We used to even go there sometimes if we'd got no money and ask for cracklings, and all the cracklings they used to push off at one side. You could get 'app'orth, I suppose, and sometimes you could get them for nothing, you know. I used to enjoy the cracklings off the fish and it was nice.
>
> Norman (born 1919)

Notes

1. Frank told me that in those days you would be lucky to eat chicken.
2. 12½p.
3. From Commercial Road to Cable Street.
4. In Hessel Street off Cannon Street Road.
5. Jo Asenine from Cable Street.

7

KEEPING CLEAN

It would be no exaggeration to say that being a working-class housewife was a full-time job. Women exhausted themselves in the daily battle against soot and dust using their only resource – elbow grease. Relaxation was something most housewives could only dream about. Mothers drummed home the importance of maintaining standards of cleanliness:

> We were poor but we were clean. They were clean and we were taught to be clean.
>
> Lizzie (born 1927)

Neighbours would notice if other people did not whiten their doorsteps *every day* with chalk. This was also a good opportunity for a chat:

> All the old girls out there, me Nan and all them used to whiten their steps.
>
> Kathleen (born 1934)

Cleanliness meant decency: Grace found it difficult to say directly how her family reacted to the news of her unplanned pregnancy, but from what she said it was a clearly a blow to their self-respect and standing:

> We was a clean band, our family. My Aunty Rose was very clean.
>
> Grace (born 1927)

One of the last things her mother had done before she died was to make sure she had washed her lace curtains by way of putting her affairs in order.

Mothers in large households could not possibly get through all the chores on their own. They had to delegate to their daughters:

> No one had fitted carpets – you had mats and those mats used to be picked up every day, brushed, and then, like, you all had your job: one would do the mat, one would sweep the floor and you didn't have 'Flash' and a mop to mop it, you got down on your hands and knees.
>
> Lizzie (born 1927)

The wooden toilet seat had to be scrubbed, the hearth blackened with lead, and the knives and forks cleaned with emery paper. The landing and communal stairs were washed down with carbolic solution, not forgetting the window sills.

Perhaps the most arduous task of all was clothes washing. This took up the whole of Monday in most households. Despite the fact that washing machines were invented in 1913, none had reached the home of the working-class East Ender:

> The worst day I used to hate when I used to go home from school of a dinner time was a Monday. Monday dinner time when your mother would be doing the washing in the corner of the kitchen in the copper – big fire. The smell of the dirty washing – oh, I used to *hate* that.
>
> Ernie (born 1913)

On washing day, a meal of leftovers late in the evening was all many mothers could manage. First they had to heat the water for the washing in the copper or on the stove:

> They'd bring a big pan of water on top of the stove and turn it up. They'd shake this carbasol over it – it was ground soda – they'd chuck that in and you'd have a great big lump of sunlight soap and a scrubbing board and you'd put it down and chuck it in this big thing near the outside tap and let it run and run and run.
>
> Grace (born 1921)

Kathleen remembered watching her grandmother at work. She used to take in washing for other people and do it in her own home:

> She had to use all the old blues' – I watched her – it was always pure white – *violent white* wasn't it, Bob. I've still got her board – you know the old scrubbing boards they used to have, I've still got it out there.
>
> Kathleen (born 1934)

> Well, when we used to do washing, we used to rub it down the board, turn it inside out, wash it again, then boil it up in the copper, so I mean it was hard work ... then it was rinsed in a big bath of cold water, and then it used to go through a great big wringer with rollers. One would put it through and the other one would do the mangle and then it used to be hung up to dry and before it was ironed it was all mangled again – yeah, it was two of yous would hold the sheets and fold them and then one would turn the wringer again [for] the towels, the tea towels.
>
> Lizzie (born 1927)

Rubber buttons were best:

> In the end she got herself a mangle but it was one of them with great big wheels and all the buttons on the shirts used to crack-she used to spend her time sewing the buttons on.
>
> Grace (born 1921)

People without a yard had problems when it came to drying their washing. In many flats they were not allowed to leave washing out on communal washing lines overnight, and there was little enough space indoors as it was. The 'excellent facilities' for drying the household washing replaced the double washing line with a pulley which women had used in the tenement flats. However, the council made a rule that tenants should not hang washing in the yard on Sundays.

Many women resorted to public washhouses or the 'bagwash'. They put all the washing into a bag and paid for it by weight. Lizzie's mother always rinsed the washing when it had returned from the bagwash, just for good measure. Alternatively women trudged up to the local baths to do their washing themselves:

> If we had a foggy day and a typical pea-souper, she used to push the pram to Ratcliffe, right along by Free Trade Wharf. Prior to that she'd to go along to Betts Street Baths ... them women in there had rubber aprons on where they used to keep themselves dry and it was like a Turkish bath – wringing wet they were.
>
> Ron (born 1921)

And finally there was the ironing. You had to heat the flat irons on the gas:

> You had two irons and you put one on the gas and that was hot and while you were ironing, the other one was hotting up. You had a cloth to put round the iron to hold it with.
>
> Lizzie (born 1927)

It was all too easy to burn oneself by mistake:

> She had a piece of old towelling and she'd rub it (the iron) on like, there, burning her hands and that.
>
> Grace (born 1921)

Left: A trip to the washhouse. A woman wheels her washing to the washhouse in the 1930s. She is also taking her own washboard. (Copyright Tower Hamlets Local History Library)

Below: Women at an ironing press, Betts Street washhouse, *c.* 1930. (Copyright Tower Hamlets Local History Library)

Just as Monday was clothes washing day, Friday was traditionally bath day:

> Before the bathroom, my sisters used to bath me every Friday in the tin bath in front of the fire [laughs].
>
> Ernie (born 1913)

Every member of this large family had their bath in the same water because of the effort needed to fill the bath from the tap in the yard.

> If you wanted a bath you had to go down with a bucket and fill it up and warm it up on top of the gas.
>
> Dolly (born 1912)

Whoever was last had drawn the short straw.
Bill came from a smaller family and so could enjoy a nice hot bath:

> I know we used to go down to the gas works down the end of the street there and get twenty eight pounds of coke and make the fire up and plenty of hot water for the bath – no trouble really, it was all wrong when you come to consider the twenty first century where everything is wonderful, they tell me, but it was quite reasonable at the time.
>
> Bill (born 1926)

Norman had baths outside in the summer. It was his father's job to scrub him clean:

> Our bath used to be an old tin – a great big tin, and in summertime we had a big barrel out in the yard, and they used to chuck us in there and give us a scrub one at a time. It was alright, it was a bit rough, you know, but then we was clean, we was always scrubbed well.
>
> Norman (born 1919)

Bath night was also an opportunity for a hair wash and eliminating nits. During the rest of the week, people had to make do with a 'wash down' or visit the public baths.

> We used to have to run errands to get our money. We used to go to Betts Street swimming baths every evening, no, not every evening, only girls – say Monday, Tuesday, Wednesday. And you'd get a towel and a penny for going swimming – we all loved it. It was the only way we got a bath.
>
> Lilly (born 1925)

> We never grew up with a bathroom, we used to go down Betts Street and have a bath down there, I think it was a penny or tuppence to have a bath down there. All families done it, the true ones of the East End, the old ones that are here.
>
> Peggy (born 1920)

While they were a step up from the tin bath at home, the local public baths were hardly a way of pampering the body:

> You got your towel down there – bit hard! But it didn't make no difference. You didn't have no scented soap.
>
> Peggy (born 1920)

> Well, I mean I wasn't far from the local baths, they were only two, three minutes from my house, so I'd go to the local baths. Tuppence for a bath, thruppence for – well two tier. There was tuppence and thruppence. For thruppence you had two towels! That's a fact that! Like boards, they were! But the thruppenny ones were a bit softer.
>
> Tom (born 1923)

People were at the mercy of the attendant who controlled the water supply to all the baths. Hot and cold came out of the same tap:

You didn't run the water, they pumped it in. You went in, you had a number on your door but someone might be a bit cocky and they'd say, 'Put water in number five' – they'd be having a laugh and you'd get all cold water coming in.

Tom (born 1923)

Since washing clothes was such a lengthy chore, most people changed their clothes weekly rather than daily:

I mean, really, when you think of it, you had your knickers on for nearly a week and really, none of us smelled—unless we all smelled the same!

Lizzie (born 1927)

People had to make do with whatever was to hand for their personal hygiene:

I mean to be honest, you never had toilet rolls. For years you'd cut the paper up and put it on the paper hook or the metal or the bit of string and you used newspaper to wipe yourself with.

Lizzie (born 1927)

Women made their own sanitary protection from old towelling or rags:

And they used to boil 'em all up and you shared the rags as you come on, and my Mum gave me this rag, and she rolled it up and it was like a bolster between your legs. And she gave you two pins to pin on your vest back and front and from that day on, you always had holes in your vest where you pinned it. And everyone was the same.

Lizzie (born 1927)

One of the greatest preoccupations of people's lives was the problem of vermin. Most people kept a working cat to keep down the mice and rats:

There was a woman who used to take cats that had kittens in, old Mrs Plum and cos the people from the RSPCA they used to come and collect them, Mrs Plum, yeah. If your cat was bad or you didn't want it no more, you carried it down Mrs Plum's.

Tom (born 1923)

Many families drowned the unwanted kittens in the copper or in the toilet.

People were bound to come into contact with others infested with nits, bugs or fleas and it was next to impossible to keep them under control. Bugs were endemic in the buildings and defied people's best efforts to eradicate them:

When we come out of this three bedroom and went into this flat, when me and my sister went a-bed, we woke up and we had all bug bites over us.

Lizzie (born 1927)

There were some people who used to be running alive with them. Bugs – them days, oh it was terrible. And they weren't nice – they smelled terrible. They stank ... because they used to feed off of humans, you know. When you was at school, and – well, we all had 'em but you'd see some people were a bit more than others you know, and some would be terrible. You'd look at the back of their neck. It'd be all bug bites and flea bites:

Norman (born 1919)

In the old slums bugs thrived on picture frames, in skirting boards and behind wallpaper:

That's why you never had wallpaper on your walls. They used to distemper it. It was like emulsion paint. Cos if you had wall paper and the bugs got behind, it'd breed, you know.

Lizzie (born 1927)

Every year, Lizzie's mother scoured the home from top to bottom in an effort to eradicate the bugs.

This involved disinfecting the skirting boards and iron bed springs and taking out all the flock from the bedding, spraying it with disinfectant and stitching it back in its covers again:

> And my Mum, every Spring, she had this great big galvanized bath and she used to, every bed, she used to undo it, tip all this flock in this galvanized bath.
>
> Lizzie (born 1927)

It is sobering looking back now in our age of modern conveniences to realise how much time and energy was required to do the housework and washing in those days of appalling housing and overcrowding:

> Oh it was – often I sit here now and I say to myself, 'How did the parents ever manage – the mother especially!'
>
> Ron (born 1921)

Tom spoke for many when he reflected on his mother's life:

> Oh she worked! Oh she worked tremendously, not only her but hundreds of them, you might as well say thousands of people in that day, they worked hard, you know for the family. I mean they never stopped.
>
> Tom (born 1923)

Notes

1. Reckitts or Jeyes Blue – chemicals to bleach the white washing.

8

HEALTH

Most of the people who contributed to this book were young working adults in 1948, the year the NHS came into being. How had they coped with illness before that? For people who take comprehensive, state-financed health care for granted, it is difficult to imagine what people did if they could not afford to pay for their treatment.

The influenza pandemic of 1918-1919, which killed over twenty million people worldwide, took its due toll on the people of Wapping. George could remember Dr Arthur, who he described as a distinguished Victorian gentleman, always elegantly dressed, complete with black leather bag. He had worked tirelessly in the Wapping area against the 'flu but his fee was well beyond the means of ordinary people. Grace Foakes describes a woman aptly named 'Mrs Saint', a qualified doctor, who gave her services free.[1] At that time, she was so overwhelmed with patients queuing up to see her that she employed a maid just to open the door.

Infectious disease was the biggest killer. Germs spread like wildfire in the overcrowded dwellings, making short work of babies, undernourished children and people with poor immunity. Since there was no cure for most infections in those days, many common conditions were life threatening. Pneumonia was not just the 'old man's friend' – it killed people of all ages.[2]

Records from St George's in the East Workhouse Infirmary between 1917 and 1923[3] list the reasons for admission during that period. TB was perhaps the commonest.[4] Infections of the skin and eyes[5] and gangrene were also recorded. Other patients were brought into hospital for what would strike a modern doctor as minor conditions – scabies, impetigo, carbuncle and conjunctivitis:

> My brother got, when he was a little boy he got erysipelas in his face [also known as St Anthony's fire] and they had to keep him in the hospital for two or three days, and we couldn't wait for him to come home.
>
> Annie (born 1925)

A shockingly large number of babies and young children were taken into hospital because of malnutrition. These infants and toddlers were not able to grow properly and developed deformed bones from rickets. Many babies died before they were a year old.[6]

Practically everybody living in the twenties and thirties would have known somebody who suffered from TB. It was so widespread that it was sometimes called 'the white plague'. Janet had the misfortune of growing up with a mother who had TB:

> They treated her for TB for years. She used to go away to the sanatorium for three months at a time, left home, left us to, you know … maybe me father was alive for some of the time. But over St George's Hospital they had two wards, number one and number two for TB patients, so she was in there … there was one [sanatorium] on the Isle of Wight somewhere, Colchester and all different places. I mean in those days when you were kids they were miles away.
>
> Janet (born 1921)

Family members in close contact with TB were sent to a local TB clinic (run by the local authority) where they received free treatment:

'Mrs Saint', a doctor who practised during the First World War and during the influenza pandemic.

One of my sisters (cos the prevalent thing in those days was TB, same as cancer is now, TB was in those days) and one of my sisters had a touch of TB and we all had to go to a place in Mercer Street – it's not there any more and we all had to be checked out. And we had to use all our own cups and all that.

Ernie (born 1913)

At the corner of Mercer Street which is where King David Lane is, there used to be a clinic for TB, and he used to have to go over there and he used to get the cod liver oil and malt there free.

Ada (born 1909)

They were advised on how to prevent the disease from spreading:

And when we went away we had to be careful where we went. When I went from St Peter's to the holiday camp in the school holidays, I was always stuck in one of the huts, not in the tent.

Janet (born 1921)

Good nursing care, fresh air and a good diet were the best that could be offered to combat most diseases. Infectious diseases of childhood such as diphtheria, measles, whooping cough and scarlet fever were major killers. In Janet's family as in most others, death was no stranger:

There were originally fourteen but only eight survived. The others all died in infancy before we were born.

Janet (born 1921)

Jack's brother was admitted to St George's in the East Hospital with infected mastoids at the age of thirteen and subsequently died from this condition.[7] In those days, a relatively minor graze could turn out to be fatal. Janet described what had happened to her father:

He was only fifty-nine when he died ... but apparently what must have been, he was a diabetic and they never diagnosed it, but he fell and grazed his elbow on one of the boats and came home, got it bathed and me mother didn't have any iodine in the place at the time. He did it on Monday, he went into the hospital, I think, St George's Hospital that used to be here. He went into the hospital Wednesday, he was dead Saturday night – gangrene.

Janet (born 1921)

Many children were born with incurable conditions:

I think nearly all my mother's sisters lost a child with heart trouble.

Lilly (born 1925)

Lilly shared a room with her sister who died of valvular heart disease when Lilly was only eight years old. The feeling of helplessness as she watched her sister suffering made a lasting impression on her:

I can remember her sometimes of a night time, she'd be up with pain.

Lilly (born 1925)

The young woman eventually died in St George's Hospital at the tender age of nineteen, and her body was brought home in her coffin until the funeral, as was the custom for Protestants and Catholics alike:

They all did – everyone in the street, when anyone died, they was laid out in the front bedroom.

Lilly (born 1925)

Nellie recalled that when her young brother died, the family had difficulty persuading the hospital authorities to allow them to bring the body home. Eventually her mother succeeded on condition that the coffin was sealed to prevent the smell of decomposition from spreading:

They wouldn't let me Mum have him home. But there was a man – undertaker – Tadman's. Well he said to me Mum, he said 'I'll show you how to put the lid on and take it off.'

Nellie (born 1916)

Catholics in Wapping kept up the great Irish tradition of the wake. Family members kept a vigil for a week or longer, so that there was always at least one person watching over the body all round the clock. In some houses there was a white sheet covering the window to show outsiders that there was a coffin in the home and, according to Ethel, some people covered their mirrors. Friends and relatives came by for 'a good old drink, a fair old chat and chin wag':

You'd have five candlesticks and they'd burn on the coffin ... we had five candles, and when they died, they used to go round the people borrowing the candlesticks for the wake, and you used to get people coming up, and you'd have a chat, and they'd have a few drinks while the other person was laying in the coffin.

Ted (born 1926)

Nearly everybody in Wapping used the one undertakers' firm, Tadman's, which had been going for three generations.[8] According to Alexander Gander, young Alf, who was the third generation of Tadman, was quite a character. At a funeral he would say out of the side of his mouth 'You don't look too well, Tom' or 'You're next, Dick!' Old Alf had had many nasty experiences when burying local prostitutes in Cable Street (a short distance from Wapping). He always insisted that the pimps pay before the burial and made them go and borrow money from their friends before taking the coffin to the hearse. Once he had been paid, Alf would hand the cash to his coachman for safe-keeping. He had learnt from bitter experience not to run the risk of being 'turned over' on the stairs by the pimps trying to get the cash back when he returned to the house to collect his tools and trestles.

Giving the dead person a proper send off was a top priority. Even the poorest people spared no expense for a funeral. Crowds of people poured out onto the streets to pay their last respects:

The Catholics all got buried at Leytonstone[9] and the main one was Tadman, and he used to have the horses with the big black plumes and lovely carriages.

Ted (born 1926)

Lilly's sister was also given a grand funeral in 1933:

> And I can remember, my mother, I told you, she was on very poor wages. I don't know how she ever paid for it, but my sister's funeral cost £18! And she had coaches and horses – two lots to cover the hearse, and we went in the coaches. This was all the way to Leytonstone. I don't know where or how she got the money for it. Insurance, probably – must have had some kind of insurance. Well they used to put them in for a penny didn't they ...
>
> Lilly (born 1925)

In *My Part of the River,* Grace Foakes describes how the undertaker, presumably Mr Tadman again, would help poor families out:

> In the case of a very small baby, where the family had no money, for a small consideration, the undertaker would place the baby in with an adult corpse. Nobody in the dead man's family was any the wiser.

If a patient pulled through the acute stages of an illness, they would more than likely be sent away to a convalescence home. This could be both alienating and frightening for a child:

> My middle sister, she was going to convalescence once and it was a Catholic home. Course when they got down there, a couple of kiddies my sister saw, she started bawling her head off, *she* didn't want her hair cut and *she* wasn't going to wear a long dress.
>
> Mary (born 1912)

At that time people believed that hair sapped the patient's strength when fighting off a feverish illness. Mary's mother managed to take her sister away – but not without a fight!

Before the introduction of vaccinations and antibiotics, disinfection and isolation were the main methods used to prevent infections from spreading. Grace Foakes writes that the patient was sent to an isolation hospital, and their room and clothing fumigated with sulphur candles. The windows were sealed up, the bedding put into big ovens and nobody was allowed into the room for fourteen days. When Annie and her sisters caught scarlet fever, they were all sent to an isolation hospital in Palmer's Green, a long way from Wapping, and poor Annie was lonely, waiting for her mother to visit.

There were various methods of treating infections. Ted, who suffered from boils, usually tried to make them burst by placing a kaolin poultice over them.

He also explained another method which he had heard of:

> Well, they get a bottle and they fill it up with steam, and they plunge it onto the boil, and the vacuum draws out all the poison, but you can't get the bottle off so they have to break it, cos it's stuck isn't it. You've got a vacuum and it goes 'wallop'. What they do is break the bottle and you've got all the poison that was in the boil.
>
> Ted (born 1926)

Doctors frequently resorted to surgical treatments. Croup and diphtheria were common, and hospital wards had a constant flow of patients like this:

> My sister, she had the croup and what they done was a tracheotomy – they put a pipe into her throat cos she couldn't breathe, and it allowed her to get on, and where it was sewed up, right in the centre of her throat, she's got a round disc where they put the pipe in.
>
> Ted (born 1926)

Annie could relive every detail of the trauma of having her tonsils removed at the age of twelve. Her mother took her to a clinic in Stepney and left her with the surgeon for the day:

> I was twelve and I had little budding boobs, you know, that you didn't take any notice of, but anyway, they put a towel round my waist – no niceties there at all, which was general then in those days. No 'Are you alright, my love?' and 'You'll be alright, don't worry' all that just wasn't done, and I was standing there with a towel round my waist – no clothes on.
>
> Annie (born 1925)

She did not recall having any pre-medication to prepare her for the operation:

> Then without any more ado, I went into the theatre and was plonked on a table with a huge gas mask plunged over my face.

The terror of the anaesthetic mask had a profound effect on Annie and the anxiety all flooded back when she had to put on her gas mask during the Second World War.

In general, people were fearful and suspicious of hospitals, and they often referred to being admitted to hospital as 'going away':

> I caught scarlet fever there [on holiday]. My Mum brought me home and I was nursed in Tower Buildings – I never went away.
>
> Ada (born 1909)

Mary blamed neighbours for not keeping quiet when her brothers were ill, which prevented the family from keeping them at home:

> By all accounts, whatever was wrong with them, they had these two lumps come up, and someone round here at the time with a big mouth was putting it around they had diphtheria.[10] And they come and took them away.
>
> Mary (born 1912)

The children were admitted to the Homerton Hospital which was rather nearer to home than many of the isolation hospitals. When one of the boys died, however, the family blamed the hospital:

> And the one, nearly five, he died because he fretted. And this one, thank God, we got him home.
>
> Mary (born 1912)

'Alleged lunatic', 'mental deficiency', 'imbecility', 'nervous debility', 'mental weakness', 'melancholia' – these were some of the labels attached to the mentally ill who were sent into hospitals all situated a long way out of Wapping.[11] These institutions superseded the asylums which had been established in the nineteenth century in more central areas of London.

Patients were still being sent to the outskirts of London when St Georges in the East closed down in 1956. Some patients might have initially been sent for assessment to the more local St Clement's Hospital.[12] People afflicted by mental illness were frequently put away for years, and sometimes for the rest of their lives:

> My father, he went a bit funny in the head; me mother had his hair cut and he went mad, and he was sent to Bexley Heath – I suppose it was a mental home then. He was there for years. We used to go up there every Sunday, one of us, well, two of us, always used to go up every Sunday to see him. That's how he ended up.
>
> Elsie (born 1913)

Hospitals (whether voluntary or Poor Law hospitals) had their own systems of funding. Very poor people could be admitted to a Poor Law hospital provided they passed a rigorous means test. St George's in the East Hospital was established in 1871 and, like many other Poor Law hospitals or 'infirmaries', originally adjoined the parish workhouse. It had a mortuary and a nurses' training school. Although the workhouse was closed at the beginning of the twentieth century, people still associated it with the hospital:

> People went down there to die, no disrespect. It was noted for that. Me Gran went in there but me Gran come out, but they mostly [didn't] – that's why they called it 'The Infirmary' – if you went in, you never come out, the old people.
>
> Jack (born 1924)

Some people could not even bear to use the word 'hospital':

> The hospital – it was called 'St George's – we used to call it 'The Infirmary', or if not people would say, 'he's down below'.
>
> Ron (born 1921)

St George's in the East began as a general hospital which dealt with most conditions. In 1930 it had 406 beds, including children's and maternity services, a TB ward and an Accident and Emergency department. One of the commonest casualties was a docker or boatman who had fallen in the river:

> The river mud was lethal because there were all the factories down the river, so when they fell in the river they were rushed into hospital *post haste* to have their lungs pumped out. They all knew on the river to get them in quick. They came and had their lungs pumped out and being tough men they'd say 'Fine, duckie, I'm alright'.
>
> Pam (1956)

When St George's was bombed in 1941, patients were evacuated to Winchmore Hill. After the war and the post-war decrease in the local population, it became more like a cottage hospital for people who mainly needed nursing or non-acute services. Pam remembered being asked to take one of the long-term residents out while she was working there as a hospital almoner:

> There was one lady, I think her name was Monica. I remember she was toothless. I can see her face – very short, cropped, white hair; she'd been in this ward for some time.

Monica was longing for a Guinness and somehow managed to persuade Pam to take her to a pub. The hospital was gradually wound down and closed in 1956 and finally demolished in 1963. People in Wapping were up in arms when the hospital was shut down but Pam felt it was inevitable:

> Being a dockland area, as the shipping came in, all the bridges had to go up.[13] So of course when the bridges went up, ambulances couldn't get through, so there were real problems of access.
>
> Pam (1956)

St George's had been a focal point for the community in Wapping and people talked of it very highly:

> Wonderful hospital! And the matron, she used to come down Choppin's Court and she used to go up to the station, we'd see her come along, it was like Queen Mary – it was wonderful – always dressed in grey, and sometimes she'd have a white hat on – she looked lovely! And a good woman. She run that hospital, it was spotless, it was clean, it was wonderful.
>
> Lilly (born 1925)

The vast, square wards, with their coal fires were originally named 'Faith', 'Courage', 'Mercy', 'Truth', 'Nightingale' and 'Honour'. From the windows, patients could gaze out at the ships in the docks. Jack's mother was a ward orderly and sang Sister's praises when describing her inspections of the ward with her white gloves on:

> Sister Felix, she'd come round, get her to pull the beds out – she used to look underneath the beds.
>
> Jack (born 1924)

Another part of Jack's mother's routine was to buy snuff for Dr Carver, the chief surgeon.[14] Pam was very struck with the friendliness of the hospital. People from many walks of life such as the police and dock customs officers were always popping in to share local news with the staff.

Although there was a strict hierarchy, there were perhaps fewer barriers than there might have been in larger hospitals.[15] The doctors had their own dining room where they enjoyed waitress service from local women, but there was also a lot of general socialising.

Wapping attracted nurses from Ireland, who lived in the nurses' home adjoining the hospital. Pam remembered being interviewed by an Irish Sister who welcomed her to Wapping. When she said she would not be staying very long, the Sister said, 'Oh, you'll stay, me dear, you can't get away; it gets into your bloodstream!' Other professional staff such as physiotherapists and occupational therapists were generally 'nice young ladies' who went home to the West End every day after work.

Both at St George's in the East and at the London Hospital the patient or the patient's family had to submit to means testing before they had any treatment:

I can remember paying to go to St George's, because I broke out in boils and every time I went there I had to pay sixpence. [16]

Ted (born 1926)

Some families, like Dolly's and Sal's, had joined the Hospital Savings Association, an insurance scheme for hospital treatment.

If you had a minor or common condition you generally went to St George's. The London Hospital, on the other hand, was a centre of excellence, dealing with the more complicated or difficult cases. In those days people had nothing but praise for the London Hospital – after all, King George V himself had been nursed there in 1928!

The London, that was the *best* – that was the number one hospital in the country! As kids, walking up Philpot Street from Watney Street, you come to the London, you'd say 'That's it' and we don't talk no more ... because that's how you respected it, because they had balconies where the public – the inmates used to be, you know. In the summer time they'd push the beds out on the verandas and that's how it was, you wouldn't talk no more. The matrons, you'd see 'em, they had blue uniform on and they had epaulettes on it, oh they had white hats – they were something to look at!

Ron (born 1921)

Self-employed or unemployed men, women and children, were not covered at all by Lloyd George's National Insurance Act:

When I used to go to the doctor, before we had Dr Leahy, Dr Korn and his surgery was above a chemist in Cable Street, and you had to take the half a crown before they see to you. You had to pay that which was a lot of money.

Bob (born 1933)

Alternatively, there were doctors outside the 'panel scheme' who worked in charitable institutions:

We used to have a sixpenny doctor, didn't we. We used to go to the Mission up in Commercial Road, and there was another one in Leman Street, a sixpenny doctor.

Ada (born 1909)

Most doctors ran dispensaries from their own 'doctors' shops'. People usually came away from a visit to the doctor with a bottle of medicine which was included in the cost of the visit – a pricey 2s 6d in the 1930s. Calling the doctor out was the last resort for poor families:

It cost half a crown for the doctor to come home to you, so your mother done most things herself.

Lizzie (born 1927)

Of course they used to do their own home remedies. The only one [was] Harry – he was very bad with pneumonia. I can remember him in the corner in Tower Buildings in a pram and a cover over him with the steam over him. He had the doctor home then, he did.

Ada (born 1909)

Paying for a home visit could lead to mistrust of the doctor's motives. Dolly, who was in the Hospital Savings Association, suspected that her doctor was trying to make money when she visited her son with gastroenteritis several times on the same day. Some doctors waived the fee if they knew that the patient could not afford to pay.

People had vivid memories of their doctors, many of whom continued to practise in the area for several generations. GP practices were often family businesses and many of the practitioners in the area were related to each other. The Drs Lipman, for example, were husband and wife.[17] Dr Lipman (husband) was spoken of with affection but little respect:

He always used to have everything what you had!

Elsie (born 1913)

Dr Lipman had his surgery at the corner of Glamis Road and he was a character amongst people because if you went in with a bunion, he'd say, 'Oh what you using for it?' You'd say, 'So and so.' 'Oh, I'll have to try that and see if it's any good!'

Ron (born 1921)

There would often be a long wait in the crowded waiting room:

You used to have, you know, a long chat, didn't you, and you used to go up there and wait, wait your turn. You'd have someone to talk to – you knew everybody else who was waiting.

Elsie (born 1913)

Dr Leahy, who carried on for many years after the war, was 'a bit of a tartar':

He'd walk in that pub, the Old Star, just to see who was in there who he's put on the sick! And they all used to run out of the other door! He'd say 'I've caught yer!'

Kathleen (born 1934)

There was Dr Barrett, he was an Irish doctor, he was lovely, he was always drunk when he come and see you, but he was *lovely*!

Mary (born 1912)

There was one doctor who was revered by all – so much so that she was nicknamed 'The angel of Cable Street'. This was Dr Hannah Billig. Dr Billig was born in Spitalfields to Jewish parents and started practising in the East End in 1927, when she took on a large number of patients from Wapping. She moved to premises in Cable Street in 1935 (where there is now a blue plaque on the building) and apart from a spell in the Indian Army during the War, worked there continuously until her retirement in 1964. Lilly was one of her patients:

Well, you sat outside in a room and no matter what time you went, you sat and you took your turn. And even if it was 'til ten o'clock at night she'd still be there seeing to them ... all my life she was wonderful.... Tell you what sort of doctor she was, you rang her, she'd be down. One Sunday, she came down to my Julie three times – she was a baby, she was hot, sweating – anyway, I said to the doctor after she got a little bit better 'What was you looking for?' She said 'Meningitis'. But that's how caring she was, she was very good.

Lilly (born 1925)

Ron remembered Dr Billig visiting his father when he was having a heart attack which he survived. Afterwards, whenever she passed him or a member of the family in her small car, she would give a little toot of recognition.

Most patients had free treatment from Dr Billig, unless they could afford to pay for it. Ethel's mother-in-law paid for frequent home visits from Dr Billig but according to Ethel, she was relatively well off. Bob described a typical consultation with her:

She'd say 'Bob, have a fag before we start', and I'd have one of hers or she'd have one of mine! Then she'd have a couple of puffs and then she'd go 'Now what's the problem?'

Bob (born 1933)

Lilly reckoned that Dr Billig saved her life, thanks to her excellent clinical acumen:

During the War, when I was fourteen, I worked in a sack firm. Well, they reckoned that I must have scratched myself and the spores, the anthrax was from one of the sacks from a foreign country.

Lilly (born 1925)

Just after the end of the war she went on to develop an infection on her arm:

Coal-black scab. And what happened was, it made me feel ill and I was in bed and my husband accidentally knocked a bottle of medicine over what the doctor had given me – smashed it. Fate! He went to the doctor's

Dr Hannah Billig who practised from No. 198 Cable Street from 1935-64. She was well loved by her patients, many of whom were residents of Wapping. She was nicknamed 'the angel of Cable Street'. (Kind permission Michael Billig)

to get another one. So she said 'How's the arm?' so he said 'Well there's red streaks going up there', so she said 'I'll be down' and she did come straight down. Twenty four hours, could have been dead. She give him a paper and he only had a motorbike then 'Go to Boots' – it was in Aldgate – 'Get this penicillin. Get her out of bed and run her up to the surgery'. Well, she put some penicillin in –I couldn't move me leg, however, it saved my life. The next day I had to go to the London Hospital. Well I got more and more doses of penicillin. I had to go in front of a classroom to show 'em all what it was, and as I said, a sister, when I go every morning for the injections, she used to say every morning 'You'll never know how lucky you are to be alive.'

Lilly (born 1925)

Dr Billig had seen anthrax when working abroad and had recognised it. One of Lilly's relatives reported that there had been warnings about anthrax in the docks when she was ill, which would have been a possible source of contagion.[18]

Hannah Billig was well known for her forthright personality. She would make her views on moral issues plain and tell people what she thought they should do:

One thing I remember about her when my husband was in the Navy and – well I was pregnant again, and I went up and I said to her 'Oh', I said 'could you help me doctor?' – 'Oh, no', she said 'he's doing *his* bit for the country' she said 'Now you do *yours*!' – so I had to have the baby.

Nellie (born 1916)

Of course abortion was illegal in those days, and agreeing to this request could have landed Dr Billig in prison like the controversial Dr Jelley who had worked in Hackney and Bethnal Green some years previously.[19] He served a three-year sentence for manslaughter, having allegedly botched an abortion.

Every night during the Blitz, Dr Billig visited people who were sheltering in the wharves:

My husband, he was ill in the shelter wasn't he, he had pneumonia, and they brought her out ... Hermitage Wharf, we used to go down there during the Blitz.[20]

Lizzie (born 1927)

In 1941, Dr Billig broke her ankle when she was blown down the steps of the shelter at Orient Wharf by an explosion. Even though she must have been in a lot of pain herself, she still carried on for a further four hours helping others who were wounded. For this she was awarded the George Medal. Ron remembered relatives of his living near the surgery telling him about her work with local prostitutes:

> Hannah Billig was busy last night, about three o'clock, the priest was outside picking up girls to go and have them medically examined.
>
> Ron (born 1921)

Following her retirement in 1964, Dr Billig emigrated to Israel, where she died in 1987 at the age of eighty-six:

> She was quite a girl, wasn't she!
>
> Bob (born 1933)

As well as the voluntary hospitals, public infirmaries and GPs, there was also a wide variety of local authority health services such as the tuberculosis and VD clinics and the school medical service. As long ago as the twenties, there were nurses whose job it was to visit schools to inspect children's hair for nits:

> We had 'Nitty Norah' come round to the school with a bowl and steel comb, and if you had nits and that, you had a letter to take home to your mother, and then the ambulance used to come to the school to take you up to go and be cleansed up at the place in Commercial Road.
>
> Ada (born 1909)

Ada had returned from a school holiday fund trip to Suffolk, 'as lousy as a cuckoo':

> Aw Gawd – and we was always all clean, only my mother was always very particular, cos my mother was in service all her life, my Mum was. Aw, she went round the school, told them off!
>
> Ada (born 1909)

Her mother always used to comb the children's hair meticulously, using a 'toothcomb', sassafras oil, a sheet of paper and straw:

> You always knew when people had nits because you could smell the sassafras oil.
>
> Ada (born 1909)

During the thirties, school doctors were expected to check vision, hearing and general health and to pick up cases of tuberculosis or children who were tuberculosis contacts and refer them to the local TB clinic. Janet received special milk at school because her mother was being treated for TB:

> The others got it in small bottles but we had it different – we had hot milk or something. Called it 'doctor's milk'.
>
> Janet (born 1921)

According to Doris, half the children in her class were so lacking energy from under-nourishment that they used to fall asleep during lessons. Sunlight treatment, which was invented in the East End of London, was given to underweight children to restore strength after a debilitating illness such as pneumonia and also prevented rickets. Weak children were also given a kind of tonic known as 'parishioners' medicine'. Lizzie longed to be told by the school doctor that she needed to go to the sunlight clinic for treatment:

> I know that perhaps I'm being big-headed but Sister Vincent [her teacher] used to call me 'Sunshine Susan' cos I was tubby as a kid, and I used to have a little fringe and that, and like, we used to have the lady doctor come every so often to school and they examined you ... and if there was anything wrong with yer, you got

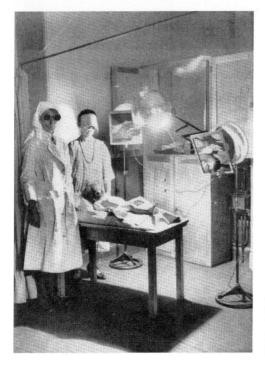

Artificial sunlight treatment. This photograph was taken at the Stepney Infant's welfare centre, *c.* 1926. Treatment would have been similar at the Wapping Pierhead clinic. (Copyright Tower Hamlets Local History Library)

a card and your mother used to have to take you to the clinic on the Pierhead, and they had a room there for sunlight, they use to call it 'the sunlight treatment' for children that were a bit poorly, and every time I used to see the doctor, I used to think 'Oh, I hope I get a card to go there, but I never did, I never got the opportunity cos I was like, all rosy-faced'.

Lizzie (born 1927)

There were several chemist's shops near to Wapping which sold medicines at a reduced rate. The pharmacists were often knowledgeable about herbal medicines which they made up themselves and displayed in large, corked, blue glass bottles. Gentian violet for external infections and oil of wintergreen for rheumatism were popular. Ipecachuana was used to make people vomit, and slippery elm for infections. The bark or stick of slippery elm could also be inserted in the vagina to induce abortion.

People believed strongly in the need for weekly 'opening medicine'. This could be liquorice powder, syrup of figs, or just cabbage water if they made it themselves. As part of the Friday-night bath ritual, parents often forced 'opening medicine' down struggling children. For good measure, they were also often made to swallow a dose of cod-liver oil with malt for extra nourishment and to prevent rickets:[21]

On Friday night we all had a bath and washed your head.

Nellie (born 1916)

And your head was tooth-combed in case you had fleas and you had a spoonful of syrup of figs whether you needed it or not!

Lizzie (born 1927)

Chemists also sold large quantities of remedies for coughs and colds making up their own cough medicines such as 'syrup of squills' and vapours for inhalation like 'Vick' or 'Friar's Balsam'. Brimstone (sulphur) added to treacle was another popular cough remedy. Practically every household slapped on the camphorated oil whenever anyone had a cough or cold:

We was never without a jar of 'Vick' indoors, never. And camphorated oil and olive oil, that was to rub – they'd always rub the soles of your feet – that was to draw it out.

Peggy (born 1920)

Mothers usually treated children for minor conditions themselves after buying what they needed from the chemist:

They used to have peroxide, and if you had an earache, they used to put a drop of peroxide in a spoon and warmed it, and you held your head over like that, and they'd put the peroxide in and it'd fizz all up, and if there was wax in there, you'd put your head over and it used to come out.

Lizzie (born 1927)

Lizzie also remembered how her mother dealt with infected cuts and splinters:

She would boil clean rags and cut 'em up in strips and cos they couldn't afford to buy, they'd put the yellow [? bassilikin] on and do it up and that used to be for drawing. If you got a splinter in, what your mother couldn't get out, you put that on and it'd draw the splinter out. My mother used to swear by Lassar's paste. [22]

Lizzie (born 1927)

In Tom's family no one ever went to see a doctor:

I can't remember a time when anyone in the family went to the doctor or went to the hospital ... she (his mother) treated it in the old-fashioned way, I suppose, I mean you never took it up with the doctors or nothing ... If you had a boil, she put a bloody hot fulmication (sic) on – a hot bit of lint put into boiling water, then she'd stick it on your neck until the pus came out.

Tom (born 1923)

Mum always treated us herself if she could, and if these two [referring to her younger brothers] was a little bit [out of sorts] then she used to blow some yellow powder down their throat and make 'em sick.

Mary (born 1912)

Lizzie's mother had her own remedy for diarrhoea:

My Mum used to mix up flour and milk and she used to give that to drink. It weren't very nice but I don't ever remember going to a doctor's 'til I got older.

Lizzie (born 1927)

Sometimes home remedies for coughs and other minor illnesses were passed down the generations. People took advice from their grandmothers. Ted's grandmother always told him to eat dripping because she thought it was good for him:

My Gran, God rest her soul, used to say, 'Eat it, it'll grease your lungs' – now I know it blocked all the arteries!

Ted (born 1926)

Often people used whatever was closest to hand. For example, bread was used as a poultice to draw out boils, and onions for coughs and colds:

We used to go hop picking years ago, and I can remember I had a cold down there, and my Mum, underneath the kiln they had a big fire, and she used to wrap an onion up in brown paper and put it in the ashes 'til it was cooked and made me eat that, and that was good for a cold. That was enjoyable, a nice onion.

Norman (born 1919)

Many children suffered the prolonged miseries of whooping cough. People believed that inhaling fumes from the gasworks or from freshly laid tarmac would help this. Ada's mother made up her own recipe for whooping cough:

If you had whooping cough, they used to do cutting up of Spanish onions, didn't they, and put foot sugar on it and let the juice go out of the onion.

Ada (born 1909)

'Foot sugar', she explained, was 'a very, very dark sugar like a toffee and they used to keep it there for twenty four hours and you'd have to drink the juice of it if you had a bad cough.'

You could treat a sore throat for next to nothing:

I only remember having one illness. I don't know what illness it was but I had a sore throat and there used to be an old lady lived in the corner house, she used to come up and she always used to put vinegar on brown paper on me throat and that's about the only illness I can remember.

Mary (born 1912)

Ethel suffered from recurrent quinsy.[23] Her mother made a poultice out of boiled vinegar and linseed oil which she applied to the throat in order to draw the quinsy out.

Whenever a child had a temperature, people thought that the best thing to do was to wrap them up to keep the heat in:

One sister I lost at four – she had a convulsion fit. She had pneumonia, but years ago if you had a cold or pneumonia, if you were running a temperature, instead of keeping you cool, they used to wrap you up in case you caught another cold, though I 'spose running a temperature, that's what caused the convulsion fit … If you had a bad cold, a really bad cold or that, your mother'd put wadding, you know, cotton wool, back and front on your chest, rub you in with camphor oil, and you'd have that on for weeks until your chest got better, and it wouldn't come off all at once, you'd have to take it off a bit at a time so you wouldn't catch a cold, you know.

Lizzie (born 1927)

Occasionally children kept the wadding on for the whole winter. Barbara, when she was teaching at St Peter's School in 1949, vividly recalled a child who underwent this treatment:

Some of them used to be sewn in for the winter. The parents used to put newspaper inside to keep them warm and then they used to sew their clothes on, so they never took their clothes off in the winter. Sometimes it used to involve a rather nasty smell coming from the children and the other children did not want to sit with them. And I remember one time having to interview this little boy's mother because the children wouldn't sit by him because he was so smelly.

Barbara (teacher in Wapping in 1949)

Perhaps the idea of 'wrapping up' was reinforced by the medical profession itself. When Doris' father had 'heart trouble', the doctor's orders were for him to wear a flannelette vest to keep his heart warm.

When asked to recall their views on the introduction of the NHS, most people did not seem to remember it with any particular enthusiasm. There is a variety of reasons which might account for this. Some people were too relieved to have got through the War in one piece to consider any other issues, others were too young or too self-sufficient to be regular users of the NHS. Several were in employment, so if they had needed medical care they had not had to pay for it. Others were treated by doctors such as Hannah Billig, who waived the fee when she thought it appropriate. Many families in Wapping were below the means tested threshold for paying in hospital.

While most people did not regard the introduction of the NHS as a landmark in their lives, Doris was very relieved when she no longer had to pay for treatment. She remembered bitterly how she had been asked to contribute to her father's care before the NHS. Her father was admitted for his cataract operation to a hospital in Aylesbury, where he stayed for six weeks:

But what annoyed me – my sister and I were working – not getting fantastic wages, and whilst he was there a letter came from the almoner to say to my sister and myself 'would we mind contributing to his operation?

Doris (born 1923)

According to testimony from GPs in the East End and all over the country, doctors were quickly overwhelmed by patients who had previously kept away. Both the increase in demand nationally, and the new treatments which had been developed during the Second World War rapidly pushed up the costs of the new NHS to unforeseen levels. The problems and complexities of a comprehensive state healthcare system were emerging almost from the moment of its inception.

Notes

1. *My Part of the River*, Grace Foakes.
2. Before the use of penicillin on a large scale, the mortality rate from pneumonia was 30 per cent. It dropped down to 6 per cent after: Roy Porter, *The Greatest Benefit to Mankind*, p. 457.
3. Source: London Metropolitan Archive. The information from these archives covers the period up to 1929.
4. This was sometimes also entered as 'phthisis' – a wasting disease of the lungs.
5. Such as trachoma, an eye infection causing blindness.
6. Diseases of malnutrition were recorded as 'marasmus', 'wasting', and rickets, conditions mainly seen nowadays in underdeveloped countries.
7. The mastoid process is part of the temporal bone of the skull. Infection from the middle ear can spread through the air cells in the mastoid bone to the brain causing fatal infections although this is practically unheard of in the West nowadays.
8. Alfred Tadman's undertakers set up in Cable Street in 1860.
9. About five miles north-east of Wapping.
10. Although the diphtheria vaccine was first used in 1895, it was slow to be adopted for general use. Roy Porter, *The Greatest Benefit to Mankind*.
11. Records of St George's in the East Hospital from 1917-23.
12. Built originally as a workhouse in 1848-49. The Mental Observation Unit was opened in 1933 and finally closed in 2007.
13. The dock bridges, not the river bridges.
14. Dr Carver worked at St George's in the 1920s.
15. Because of the hierarchy perhaps, medical students enjoyed the opportunity to play tricks on the consultants. Ted enjoyed reminiscing about medical student pranks during his time at the London Hospital as a handyman during the war, repairing bomb damage:

   'But the worst thing they done, at that time, they had a surgeon that was head of all the hospital, and they got plaster of Paris and they plastered all his phones up and left them, and he was rather hot under the collar.'

   The students also managed to get a car up on the roof of the London Hospital:

   'A Ford Square – an old 1938 car, they got it in the lift and took it up on the roof! Well at that time we had no cranes, so we had to take bottles up there and burn it.'

   Ted (born 1926)
16. Means testing at the London Hospital was stopped when a private wing was built in 1937.
17. He was an Irish Jew and his wife was a Catholic. The Drs Lipman lived above the shop from about 1925 to just before the Second World War. Dr Reidy's time in Wapping spanned the entire period between 1914-39. He practised in Old Gravel Lane with his wife.
18. Every shed in the docks had to have compulsory warnings about anthrax which could be caught from dry hides imported from America for the leather and tanning industry in Bermondsey. There were very occasional cases of anthrax in the docks. Protective clothing and disinfectant were provided for those at risk.
19. Dr Jelley (1866-1946), a colourful eccentric who practised in Hackney.
20. This must have been before they were married.
21. My father's parents promised him that he would get a penny once the bottle was finished. When he earned his penny, they made him buy a second bottle with it.
22. Zinc oxide and salicylic acid with or without coal tar.
23. Throat abscess.

9

WOMEN'S HEALTH

In the first part of the twentieth century, the health of married working-class women was the worst of any group in society. Women who were on their feet working in the home for up to sixteen hours a day were prone to suffer from rheumatism, exhaustion and general debility.[1] Moreover, until the late 1930s, most working-class women had no antenatal care and only a small percentage of married women were in paid work, leaving the majority without any health insurance.

Having a baby was a risky venture in those days, and thousands of women died unnecessarily in childbirth every year. Many women were like Lizzie's mother, who started her reproductive career in 1916 and ended up with a total of thirteen children:

> My mother used to have a baby every two years or eighteen months – she had her first baby at eighteen and her last baby at forty-four.
>
> Lizzie (born 1927)

Tom reflected on the strains on his mother, and how she had 'suffered with her nerves':

> Course she had a hard life bringing up bloody nine kids of her own!
>
> Tom (born 1923)

When one of her sons was killed in the Second World War it was the last straw, causing her to have a breakdown. Not only did women have to submit to the physical suffering of relentless childbirth, but they also often had to endure the grief of bereavement:

> I lost my first one – first one was a boy, but I lost it at birth. I was a machinist and they reckoned sitting too long at a machine …
>
> Dolly (born 1912)

Until the 1930s, most working-class women had their babies at home in overcrowded, insanitary conditions. They only called a doctor if there was a serious problem. During labour, the mother was attended by a member of her family, such as her own mother or her sister, or a neighbour experienced at delivering babies. These women, sometimes known as 'handywomen', also had skills in looking after the sick and dying, and knew how to lay out the dead:

> My mother went down with that Spanish flu[2] and she was seven months pregnant, and the twins – that's my sister who is alive and my brother, they were born. You didn't have no midwives or nothing. A Doctor Reidy was in Wapping then, and there used to be a lady – she didn't pass no tests, but she was the local woman who went in and helped when anyone had a baby. And Mrs Leek and my Nan helped to deliver the two babies – they were seven months premature and when Dr Reidy come in, he picked the two babies up by their legs and he didn't even have a scale, he said 'I would say seven pound between the two of them'. And me brother – they didn't expect him to live, and my Gran, she washed him in olive oil and they wrapped him, the two twins, both of them, they wrapped 'em in cotton wool and they made a crib of a big drawer, and they put the two babies there, and me brother, he was twenty one, he got killed in the War, but me sister's still alive, she's 84.
>
> Lizzie (born 1927)

Above left: Nellie aged sixteen, 1932. She had her first baby at eighteen and her last at forty-five.

Above right: Lizzie's grandparents with the twins and an older sister, *c.* 1920. The twins, Eileen and George, were born prematurely at home. George was killed in the Second World War but Eileen lived to a ripe old age.

Mary's family was better off, so they had both the doctor and a midwife when her mother was in labour with her younger brother in 1917. There seems to have been some rivalry between them. Mary's father called the doctor because her mother was in labour:

> And course, when he come down, old Mum wasn't ready and he went back, so a little while after it started again.

This time her father came back with a midwife:

> So she stayed with Mum 'til my brother was born, then she said, 'Now you can go up for him [the doctor]' and when he come back, she, well, she told him what she thought of him, so when Dad went to pay him, he [the doctor] gave [the midwife] the money. I don't think he wanted to, but she went and bought all clothes for me brother out of that.

Mary (born 1912)

Doctors who were trying to establish themselves were keen to undertake maternity care as a way of acquiring loyal patients who were a good source of income with, usually, many more babies to come. In 1918, a doctor could earn the hefty sum of 10s 6d for, say, a breech birth occurring during the night requiring forceps. More straightforward births at night cost 5s and a day visit 2s 6d. Some women had their babies in the local 'lying in home', so called because it was the custom for a woman to rest in bed for fourteen days after having a baby. In the late thirties this cost 10s 6d.

A certain doctor who signed himself 'J.H.L.' kept a record of his attendances to women in labour both at home and in the East End Mothers Lying in Home from 1916-23.[3] Out of around 1,000 visits, Dr 'J.H.L.' dealt with frequent complications of pregnancy and childbirth, including life-threatening conditions to mother or baby. He also noted a baby afflicted with German measles, and another with spina bifida. Many of the infants were born prematurely, or were described as 'feeble' and altogether there were thirteen stillbirths. One entry, dated 23 December 1918, provides a detailed account of the doctor's visit to a woman at her home in Wapping in the middle of the night:

10 para.[4] Breech with extended legs. Patient in labour five hours, strong pains, sudden faintness and collapse. 9½lb still-born infant delivered by Sister ten minutes before my arrival. On examining, found placenta adherent and a large rent through posterior fornix. Removed placenta and did as little locally as possible. Gave 1oz brandy and Oxo 2 hourly.

Pulse 120 and feeble. Rather free haemorrhage during removal of placenta. No visible haemorrhage after.

9 AM. Pulse a little improved and patient warmer. Arranged for removal to hospital. (Hysterectomy performed at once by Dr Gordon Lay)

Grace had vivid memories of having her first baby at the local lying–in hospital in 1938. She had fallen pregnant accidentally at the age of sixteen and was bewildered and frightened by the whole experience. The worst thing of all, was 'an enema in front of all these nurses and people, because you had – it was a toilet and you sat on it and you had to keep bearing down'.

A broad abdominal binder made of strong linen was placed tightly around her belly. The 'lying in' period was thought to prevent prolapse of the womb. For some women, it was their one and only opportunity to get some rest, but many could not follow doctors' orders because they were needed at home. Once Grace had recovered from the shock of giving birth, she rather enjoyed her stay at the lying–in hospital. The doctor, who she addressed as 'Sir' came round regularly to make pleasant conversation:

I always remember, that was the first time I ever tasted minced meat in me life and I liked it! Oh, we got lovely porridge – we were well looked after … In bed for fourteen days – never had so much rest in all my life!

Grace (born 1921)

Most girls were brought up in complete ignorance of sex. Despite the fact that childbirth occurred so regularly, somehow mothers managed to hide the impending event from the other children, so that it came as a surprise. Several people had similar experiences to Ethel:

She sent us round the park. When we come back there was a new baby!

Ethel (born 1916)

After a while she learned to guess what was coming:

You always knew when you got a treat, because you got a bottle of lemonade you know, the old powdered lemonade, and you made it up with a little water – sherbet, mmm!

Ethel (born 1916)

Annie would never forget the day her younger brother was born, when she was nine years old. One day, she found her mother in bed, and in the room with her were her aunt, her grandmother and a baby. She was genuinely puzzled as to where the baby had come from:

There was my mother upstairs in bed with this gorgeous, gorgeous baby. 'That baby can't be ours!' I said to my Gran, 'It must be yours!' – 'If it's not yours, Nanny, it must be Auntie Ruth's' – and Auntie Ruth was about nineteen and wasn't married – so anyway it *was* ours.

Annie (born 1925)

Few mothers appear to have given their daughters the slightest preparation for the onset of their periods:

I was probably about twelve, I would think, and I had this bleeding, and I went downstairs and I said to my Mum 'Mum, I've got all this blood coming away from me' and I can remember this – she flushed up – embarrassment, you see.

Annie (born 1925)

Her mother showed her what to use, and delivered two words of advice by way of sex education:

> 'Be careful!' I don't know what I had to be careful about, and that was that. We never mentioned it again.
>
> Annie (born 1925)

As Lilly put it:

> Well, we was very – er, as regards sex and all that, we never – we was very backward.

Consequently, women were often wholly unprepared for what would befall them in later life. Lizzie remembered speculating with her friends, when she was a girl, about how women got pregnant:

> One of the girls, she went 'I found out how you have a baby' – and up Cable Street you had all the black men then, it was well known, there was a little colony of black men, and she said 'if a man looks into our eyes and you look into his, you had a baby!'
>
> Lizzie (born 1927)

Many parents kept their daughters under close supervision out of fear that they would bring disgrace on the family by falling pregnant out of wedlock:

> And your mother was very strict those days – half past nine at night, especially in the winter, she'd be round looking in at all the doorways seeing if they [her daughters] were going with any boys and that.
>
> Ernie (born 1913)

> I was allowed out of Wapping then, but I just had to be home by a certain time, didn't I. I had to be at home by nine at night.
>
> Kathleen (born 1934)

The social stigma of having an illegitimate child was enormous. In the earlier part of the twentieth century, a single mother ran the risk of being shut away in a mental institution for the rest of her days if she did not have the support of her family. According to Nellie, when she was a young woman having her first baby in the early thirties in the London Hospital, the policy was not to admit women to the labour ward unless they were married. The lying-in hospital, however, took in any woman regardless of her marital status:

> A lot of people were very narrow-minded in those days. I never experienced it myself – I mean, your family stuck by you didn't they, but some people like, if a girl got in trouble they'd send 'em away … cos their mothers wouldn't let 'em keep 'em you see, cos there was no social services then, like.
>
> Lizzie (born 1927)

Most women would have known how to procure an abortion, and also would have heard of people dying from abortions.[5] Foetuses were regularly found in the river:

> I remember, I mean though our mothers never talked about nothing in front of us, did they, but like, you'd pick up things like, what they were saying and – oh, I can remember, I went to school with a girl, her mother went somewhere and had a back street abortion and she died, you know. People used to take, if they was over [i.e. missed their period], they used to take pills or gin, but it didn't always work and they'd sit in a mustard bath – but it didn't always work.
>
> Lizzie (born 1927)

Grace was one of the unlucky girls who fell pregnant accidentally when she was sixteen:

> I was so naïve I didn't know what was happening to me.
>
> Grace (born 1921)

Once pregnant, she recalled that she felt grateful to the father of the child for marrying her. An abortion was out of the question in her case. Sex before marriage was regarded as disgraceful and

'The most beautiful woman people had ever seen'. This local belle came from a large family and married a Wapping boy. They ran a sweet shop which was on the site of the present Wapping Health Centre.

indecent, and marriage was the only way to salvage the situation. Abortion was something that other people did:

> Aaw – we had a chemist round the corner but we didn't really know, because being a youngster then, my Mum and them never talked about that, and my aunt Rose used to come in with some stories about this one that one and the other one … and anyway this poor woman on the end [of the street], my aunt said 'She's disgusting, she's worse than a beast in a field!' but it was something I'd gone through and I'd paid the penalty for it but I woke up too late, you know.
>
> Grace (born 1921)

Most women probably did not use any contraception. Rather, they relied on breastfeeding, the rhythm method and coitus interruptus to space their pregnancies.[6] According to a woman who lived on Cable Street:

> There was no birth control: they used to tell you to put two legs in one stocking. You had intercourse with your husband – whenever he wanted it you had it.[7]

Nearly everybody breastfed their babies quite openly. According to George, it was normal to see women suckling their babies on the streets of Wapping in the twenties and thirties. More sophisticated methods of birth control as advocated by Marie Stopes, such as douching, diaphragms, caps or pessaries, were either too expensive or downright impractical for people who did not have a bathroom.[8]

During the inter-war years, the scandalous situation regarding women's health came to the forefront of the political agenda thanks to campaigns led by Sylvia Pankhurst and other women's rights activists. From the mid-thirties onwards, several measures were introduced to increase safety levels for mothers and babies. Women were encouraged to have their first baby in hospital, and by the forties the majority of women were doing so. With a higher standard of living, the introduction of obstetric flying squads, blood transfusions, sulphonamide drugs, more antenatal care and, most importantly, the general decrease in the number of pregnancies, the health of the next generation of women was to improve dramatically.

Notes

1. This appalling state of affairs was made public in the *Women's Health Inquiry*, a survey of 1,250 working-class married mothers from all over the United Kingdom The survey uncovered high rates of anaemia, bad teeth, rheumatism, and exhaustion. *Working Class Wives, Their Health and Conditions* by Margery Spring Rice was published in 1939. The book drew attention to the vast difference in health between rich and poor and the dangers to the health of married women compared to single women or men.

2. During the influenza epidemic of 1918-19.

3. The lying in home was at Steele's Lane, Commercial Road, E1. This record was handed down to me by a colleague, Dr Andrew Dunford, to whom it was given in turn by Dr Wilkinson his predecessor, who had practised in Wapping for several decades.

    Entries include prolapse of the cord, impacted breech, eclampsia and post-partum haemorrhage. Placenta praevia, a condition where the placenta is low down in the womb and can bleed massively, was sometimes treated by inserting 'a bag' into the vagina.

4. This means the woman had already had ten children.

5. In 1934, 13 per cent of maternal deaths were the result of abortions. This is probably an underestimate, as self-inflicted abortions were often recorded as 'miscarriages' and back street abortions were performed in secret.

6. Grace Foakes mentions that women would try to continue breastfeeding for two years as a means of delaying a further pregnancy.

7. Oral history interview National Sound Archive.

8. According to Jennifer Worth, very few men could be persuaded to use a sheath. See *Call the Midwife*.

10

MARRIAGE AND WOMEN'S WORK

Do you know that I never gave or received a kiss 'til I was sixteen, when I kissed Danny Reilly [her future husband].

Lilly (born 1925)

Once married, most people's mothers gave up their jobs so that their whole world shrunk into their household. Women with large families spent all their time running the home. People remembered their mother as a continuous presence in the background doing the household chores:

Some of the women hardly went out of the area of their house.

Ron (born 1921)

Most women had no opportunity to put their feet up:

My mother worked almost from – in those days – she was up at four o'clock in the morning and she worked 'til practically midnight oil, you know, nine of us.

Tom (born 1923)

Prior to marriage, they might, like Ada's mother, have had jobs as live-in domestic servants, sometimes quite far away from home. When times were particularly hard, say, if their husband was on strike or out of work, a woman would somehow manage to find the time in the day to earn a little extra money doing piecework:

Your mother used to earn a few bob – used to take in washing for someone who went to work and it was about two pence a dozen.

Lizzie (born 1927)

She sometimes did a bit of homework you know – had stuff –trousers and that – brought home and felling them. It's without turning the edge under – I did learn it –where you sort of cross it over but it lays flat.

Janet (born 1921)

She used to pick shrimps at one time and it was very good when we had shrimps for tea and winkles and whatever.

Norman (born 1919)

Before the Great Depression there was plenty of local work. Ted's mother had met his father working on the river:

Well, my father was a deep sea sailorman, but he had a Thames sailing barge he was a skipper on. And he used to go over to Belgium and get the bottles, and then women would unload his barge ... and they'd go up a plank and from the barge up onto the shore.

Ted (born 1926)

Women at Wapping, 1949. Two women are having a chat. One is carrying firewood. (Copyright Getty Images)

The various factories in Wapping, such as Gibbs' soap factory and Alexander's tug company, employed local women as cleaners or cooks. Many women worked in the tin factory and the various sack-repairing and tarpaulin factories in and around Wapping which had originally engaged Irish women working from home. The hospital also provided local women with jobs. Doris' older sister worked as a waitress in the doctors' dining room, and Jack and Lilly's mothers, both single mothers, went out to work as hospital cleaners:

> Women got preference, when they lost their husband, to work in St George's Hospital – She done twenty five years as a cleaner, me mother.
>
> Jack (born 1924)

Being a hospital cleaner was a tough job, especially without the use of labour-saving machines:

> Scrubbing on her hands and knees seven days a week – on Sunday as well. She used to start at seven o'clock in the morning 'til two, then she'd have to go back at five 'til eight.
>
> Lilly (born 1925)

Before working as a hospital cleaner, Jack's mother had worked in one of the sack factories:

> ... there used to be a big tent factory in Wapping, Smiths, making tents for the army, and bags in 1914 for the dead. My Mum was a tent maker.
>
> Jack (born 1924)

It was easy to get a job as a sack mender because of the large warehouses storing commodities from the docks, but it was unrewarding and very hard on the hands:

> She [Dolly's mother] was a sack repairer ... years ago they had sacks to put the flour in and the sugar ... and she used to repair any holes that came into the sacks so the governor could use them again.
>
> Dolly (born 1912)

We used to make sandbags and shrouds for the bodies they found in the bombed out shelters. Some of the sacks used to come from abroad – sugar and fibre like, from coconut leaf and all that.

Lilly (born 1925)

A few women like Elsie's mother ran their own businesses. She had a successful oil and hardware shop:

Well, there's one of my sisters, she took it over first, then she went in ammunition, and then the other sisters took it over, then she was called up for telephones and then it left me mother to look after it.

Elsie (born 1913)

Mary's mother made wreaths at home which she sold in her small shop in Old Gravel Lane.

As soon as daughters left school at the age of fourteen, they went straight out to work so that they could contribute to the family income:

I left school on the Friday and I was at work on the Monday.

Peggy (born 1920)

Naturally, at such a tender age, girls found work near to home. By the 1930s, domestic service had almost become a thing of the past, except perhaps amongst the top echelons of society:

I left school at fourteen and then I went to work. And I went in the same trade as me mother – wasn't a very good trade but we were glad of it to have a job.

Dolly (born 1912)

Working in dock warehouses was, perhaps, more enjoyable than working as a sack mender. Kathleen had a job in the great spice warehouse, testing the quality of the ground pepper, cinnamon and nutmeg. Lizzie, like many other local women went to work in the British and Foreign Wharf:

We used to bottle all the gin and the whiskey and all that.

Lizzie (born 1927)

Most of the girls worked in the British and Foreign Wharf in Wapping, that's where the spirits were made into rum, whiskey and gin, and all the girls – I shouldn't tell you this, but you know the hot water bottles, the rubber ones? They used to take them in there, put them down their knickers and come out with all the whisky and the gin! Oh yeah! I've seen it a thousand times, they used to come out wearing it down their knickers!

Jack (born 1924)

The huge quantity of tobacco stored in hogsheads in Tobacco Dock was sold to the many large cigarette- and cigar-manufacturing companies in the East End. Most of their employees were women:

Godfrey Phillips, tobacconists, right at the top of Commercial Street, a big, big cigarette manufacturer's – that was my first job.

Peggy (born 1920)

Ethel described her work hand-making cigars with pride. She worked for one of the several Dutch cigar-making firms in Aldgate:

My actual job was five years' apprenticeship making cigars. You got all bits of dried leaf and they was thrown on the floor 'til they dried right out, then you got this leaf like this – it was kept moist – you could lift that up. The girls used to strip them out, then you got one half of a leaf and that half of leaf was your outside wrapper … then we put them in like a mould, wooden mould and in the press.

Ethel (born 1916)

Later she joined the Brooke Bond Tea Co.:

They give me hammer and nails – a cooper of them bleeding tea chests, I was! I'll tell yer, I've done everything!

Ethel (born 1916)

Women worked in several other light industries near Wapping, such as the Meredith & Drew cake and biscuit factory and Yeatman's fruit and jam factory at the end of Old Gravel Lane in Wapping. This later became part of the Tiptree jam company:

I used to work for Yeatman's along the Highway. And they used to have a chocolate factory in Denmark Street as well. Where I worked, it was jam and squashes and all tinned fruit, Christmas puddings, tinned puddings and all that sort of thing. But I was a hand labeller. I stuck labels on by hand. I was a piece worker. They were already printed and I used to have a big board and I used to paste it and you used to slide all your labels down and wash your jars or whatever you was labelling up and stick 'em on. Yeah, I loved it, really loved it. The people was nice and in the summer time when all the fruit used to come in season, we used to go [into] what they used to call 'the yard' and have big benches put up, and all the fruit used to be put on the benches and you'd tin 'em and they'd take 'em in the cannery and then cook 'em.

Sal (born 1925)

When they were working with lemons, the women put vaseline up their arms to prevent the juice from irritating their skin.

One of the most widespread occupations amongst Wapping women between the two World Wars was tailoring. Women often worked for small Jewish firms where they specialised in a specific part of a garment:

I used to do what they used to call 'goffering' in an underwear place – you know, when you get a pleated petticoat, all the lace round it – what they call 'goffered' and I used to do that.

Elsie (born 1913)

I had several different jobs in machining works, and I worked at underclothes making, I worked at coat making, and I used to work for a Jewish man in the tailoring, and that was before the Second World War. I used to do part of the coat, I used to do all the racing on the coats and I used to do all the sleeves and all that.

Mary (born 1912)

The 'racing', she explained, was a way of putting a pattern onto the border. Mary's sister was also an accomplished tailor:

My oldest sister – she made all our coats and there was a lady over in old Prusom Street buildings that was, she used to do all this, they used to call it, years, ago, 'lock' – net stuff, like stockinet stuff, and do all the beading work on it. My sister made me a mauve coat and it had a flap over like that and it had a little collar, an astrakhan collar on it. And she made me a hat with grey astrakhan round the rim.

Mary (born 1912)

Not everybody, however, went to work in factories or in the rag trade. Some better-educated girls obtained employment in the City:

I was fifteen in the January and I left [school] in the April and I started work in the May for that solicitor.

Doris (born 1923)

Since she never married, Doris stayed in the same job for the rest of her working life.

Before the Second World War, the marriage bar reduced a woman's employment opportunities in many walks of life:

I used to work at tailoring ... but as soon as I got married I had to leave.

Nellie (born 1916)

When anyone got married they never worked on, they wouldn't take married women on ... my sisters worked for the Ardath tobacco firm, and if you were married they wouldn't keep you on.

Lizzie (born 1927)

Whether women were accepted for work or not depended on the state of the labour market. During the thirties, when there was mass unemployment and economic recession, marriage was a good excuse for bosses to save on employment costs. On the other hand, the marriage bar was lifted when women were needed. The London Hospital, for example, had accepted some women medical students between 1918-22 when there was a shortage of men, and again during the Second World War.

Working-class women needing extra money generally fell back on cleaning jobs once they were married with children. Sal did not return to the jam factory:

I used to do office cleaning you know, which helped make ends meet. We had a good life, we've never gone without anything, we've always had a holiday.

Sal (born 1925)

Women had to get up at the crack of dawn to go to work. Dolly gave up her work in the sack factory when she got married:

When I had the children. I used to go in the hours they used to be all at school – used to be in work six am to eight am and chase all the way home to get them up to go to school.

Dolly (born 1912)

Lizzie's wedding, 1949. The groom's aunt made the cake and 'everyone in the family gave up a bit of their rations to make it'.

When children came along (hard work when they were at home) office cleaning in the morning, office cleaning in the evening when their father would be home.

Lilly (born 1925)

Lilly's life was hard, but at least she had support from her husband. Those women who were in bad marriages were often trapped in a life of misery. Without training, education or the opportunity to earn enough money to stand on their own feet, and in the absence of a safety net provided by the state, many women were completely dependent on their husbands:

Really, years ago, a lot of people put up with a lot from their husbands, because who would have kept 'em? You know what I mean?

Lizzie (born 1927)

Grace's life after her unplanned pregnancy at the age of seventeen was a tragedy. She had felt, once she had fallen pregnant, that she had had no option other than to marry the father of the child:

There wasn't no thought, it just rambled on. And I rambled with the tide, sort of thing.

Grace (born 1921)

Things rapidly turned nasty: she found herself being abused in the marriage for several decades with no possible means of escape. Her husband assaulted her when drunk, giving her serious injuries, which she did her best to hide. She did not tell anyone about it:

It wasn't done in those days…lots of women suffered this – terrible … Ribs got cracked. I just wrapped meself up. I had crêpe bandages. I used to breathe like that [demonstrating shallow breathing] cos it used to hurt, you know.

I used to crawl away and cry 'Please don't leave me' – because I'd have nowhere, no one. And the dole money in them days … they were pennies, absolute pennies.

Grace (born 1921)

Many women were introduced to the world of work when they were called up for the War effort if they chose not to be evacuated with their children and during the War, women were obliged to stay on at work after marriage whether they liked it or not. Lilly would have liked to have left the sack factory:

We couldn't get out of there once we was in. We had to stay – yeah, worked there for about six years. I got married and still done a bit of work there.

Lilly (born 1925)

From 1941 all women between the ages of eighteen and sixty had to be registered for work. They were interviewed and required to choose from a range of jobs. By 1943 nearly 90 percent of single women and 80 per cent of married women were employed in essential work for the War effort. A widening generation gap appeared between mothers and their daughters, with many young women taking on men's jobs in engineering firms or the railways and such unlikely places as the Royal Mint. Looking back, Janet considered that she had benefited from the War, and was proud of her achievements:

I had a bit of intelligence – I wanted more or less to work in an office but then worked at the BDV tobacco factory. I volunteered for the ATS February 1942: I wasn't twenty one – cos I wanted to be in a job I could pick and do something. I did train as a driver – I was a lorry driver for a while – Searchlight Unit, North London, Hertfordshire.

Janet (born 1921)

The Second World War was a significant catalyst for changing the status of women in society. The marriage bar was abolished in the public sector in 1946, and most women were able to work regardless of their marital status. Improvements in education and the creation of the welfare state led to a gradual increase in women's independence from men.

11

CHILDHOOD

Looking back on their childhood some seventy-five years ago or more gave most people intense pleasure, despite the fact that many of them were made to work from an early age. Elsie helped her mother in the family grocery shop:

> If we were caught taking a biscuit or a sweet, you'd get your hands rapped. You weren't allowed to take anything.

As a very old lady, she could still remember all the details:

> We all had our own share of work in the shop – scrubbing the counters down, scrubbing the shelves, you know, scrubbing the floors … Thursday night, that was my night – we did use to work hard!
>
> Elsie (born 1913)

Boys and girls were allocated different jobs. Collecting driftwood from the river shore and chopping it up for firewood was boys' work. Girls might have to help their mother carry the heavy shopping home from the market, or queue up at the gas works to lug the bags of coke back in a pram. On Mondays they were needed to help with the laundry. If they were lucky, they might earn a penny from their father for polishing his boots, competing with their brothers and sisters for the privilege. Older girls were expected take over from their mother if she was not well. Ada remembered going to the market with her father and brother to buy potatoes. He abandoned them with the barrow and went to the pub:

> Me and me brother, we used to trudge it home – I had the ride. None of the others had to do it – they got the poshest jobs but I 'spose there was fun in it.
>
> Ada (born 1909)

The idea of pocket money was unknown to dockers' children. Most of them did a variety of jobs and errands to earn money for treats:

> [We used to] take someone's bag round a shop up the Highway, or run round the Lane – all the shops was there – they were open late and you'd get a ha' penny off someone, or a farthing off somebody else – you would never have had much, and that's how you'd get your ha' pennies or pennies to get sweets or whatever.
>
> Lilly (born 1925)

> When we used to be little children in Jackman [House], some of the poor women used to say 'Will you go round Wakeman's' (that's the paper shop) and you used to have a twist of snuff, Wilson's, for a ha' penny, and we used to undo it and it would blow your head off!
>
> Ted (born 1926)

Some children used to do jobs on Saturdays for Jewish people living just outside Wapping, whose religion forbad them to work on the Sabbath. The Jews were good employers.

Annie and her sister. This was taken in the early 1930s on the roof of Riverside Mansions showing just how close to the docks people lived.

Groups of children, some as young as six or seven years old, formed working cooperatives to sell coke or firewood for a regular clientele:

> And I'll tell what else we used to do an' all when we were children to earn a few bob. The boys used to chop all the wood up in sticks cos you have to pay a penny for a bundle of wood to light the fire, then you'd go with one of the boys, he'd put so much wood in your hand and you'd knock on the door and people would buy it off of you. It'd be cheaper than the shop and then at the end of the day, say there was five or six of yous done it, you shared it out between yous and you'd go up the pictures for a penny, up the Penny Pictures.
>
> Lizzie (born 1927)

> Over the Hermitage¹ was a brewery, horses brewery, and when the crates got busted they used to chuck 'em in a heap and we'd go over there with our carts, collect all the wood, chop 'em up and go knocking on the houses [selling] a bundle of wood for a ha'penny.'
>
> Ted (born 1926)

Jack's cooperative made large profits – enough for the shareholders to spoil themselves silly with toffee apples:

> I used to go down Wapping with my barrow. We'd get – it used to be twenty eight pounds of coke, then fourpence, and we'd have about twenty sacks on a board and we'd come out and we'd get four shillings – about a shilling each, all the way from Wapping gasworks.
>
> Jack (born 1924)

People could remember exactly how they spent their hard-earned money:

> We'd go up to Betts Street for the baths, that was the swimming baths. Well, if you'd done well by selling your firewood, you might make tuppence, well when you come out there was a café, an Italian café, 'Mantessi'. You'd go in there, and you'd get two big doorsteps of bread and dripping and a big mug of tea for a penny.
>
> Ted (born 1926)

Nellie and her friends made a beeline for the jellied-eel stall:

> I remember going swimming and when we came out there was Tubby Isaacs, the jellied eels. We used to

come out and used to ask for a penn'orth of jelly – couldn't afford the eels – and he used to give jelly and a slice of bread.

Nellie (born 1916)

Fruit was also a treat:

> Facing The Cable there used to be a little fruit shop and like, you'd pay to go in The Cable, and you used to go in this fruit shop and you'd ask for a 'penn'orth specks' and all the apples and oranges that had gone a bit 'specky', they used to cut 'em off, and you'd get, you know, some apples and oranges for about a penny.[2]

Lizzie (born 1927)

Even better than that was getting a whole orange all to yourself. This sometimes happened when walking past the dockers whilst they were unloading produce:

> Opposite Dundee Wharf was Morocco Wharf and they used to have all the ships coming from Haifa with Jaffa oranges, tangerines and grapefruits. Well, they used to roll a big Jaffa orange out – we used to sit down and have a feast!

Ted (born 1926)

New potatoes from Jersey also came in at Morocco Wharf. At 5-6d/1b they were too dear for many families:

> But we used to stand across – there were horses and carts then – (not many lorries) with baskets that come to be loaded down, and all of a sudden the men at the top used to shout to us 'Under!' and the basket'd break open, and we'd all dive under the horses [and put them] in your pinafore. Even if you got a few it was marvellous!

Janet (born 1921)

Some children used to mooch hopefully around the wharves waiting for a treat:

> What we used to do, going round the wharves and seeing what was what, you know, asking them to bowl out the oranges when the boats come in and sometimes they've had nuts and they used to sling the walnuts or hazelnuts and we used to pick them up and have a crunch.

Ted (born 1926)

Lilly took food home. She used to:

> Get the bananas out the cases while they were being loaded – mind you they were green, but you put them in a drawer and they soon ripened up. That was St Bride's down near Wapping Station. Bananas and tomaters. Sometimes they'd drop a case, bust open – whoah! you'd have plenty of tomatoes! At Colonial Wharf, they done tea and they often, out of the crates dropped a case of tea – it'd smash, so you had the pickings of tea.

Lilly (born 1925)

> The dockies knew the kids didn't get a lot of things … And round the back they used to bring in the big bags of the peanuts – they weren't in shells but they weren't roasted, and someone'd accidentally break the thing and all the kids'd fill their pockets up with peanuts.

Lizzie (born 1927)

The dockers risked losing their jobs when they passed food to children. Janet kept away from her father when he was at work for this reason:

> He'd do his *nut* you know, working up there. And we weren't allowed to walk up there if they were at work.

Janet (born 1921)

Children mostly played outside on the streets. There was little alternative as there was not much space in the yards of the tenement blocks and even less room indoors.

Our playground was ropes hanging from the dock walls and we'd be sitting on them swinging.

Kathleen (born 1934)

Always out all the time playing. Especially in the winter – we used to love the winter, because if it was really cold, we used to get some water down a slope – it'd only take ten minutes, it'd freeze, and you'd start making a slide!

Ernie (born 1913)

Sometimes rival gangs congregated in the streets and a fight would break out, say 'the Clegg Street boys' versus 'the Reigate Street boys', but there was never any serious trouble. If boys were playing football or cricket in the yard, the caretaker would send them packing when it got to 9 p.m.

You would get a scuff alongside the eardrum or he'd chuck you out.

Ted (born 1926)

You'd play for hours, holiday time especially, and you didn't have the traffic: during the week, it was all the horses and carts because of the docks, and now and again there was a motor but not much, but no-one had cars.

And on the weekends or holiday times you had a great big rope – grown-ups had a great big thick rope – perhaps got one off the dockies – and two grown-ups would do the rope and all of us kids would skip.

Lizzie (born 1927)

Sons and daughters of the few middle-class families in Wapping enjoyed playing with their toys in large gardens. Some had piano lessons with the local teacher, and attended Brownies, Girl Guides or Boy Scouts. Lilly remembered how the only toy she was ever given met with a sticky end:

I had a treat once – I never forgot it! The matron in the hospital gave my mother a beautiful – we always laugh about this – a little baby doll. It was dressed in knitted blue. I can see the colour of it, blue like the lid of that butter dish. And she walked in and give it to me, and my sister promptly got it, hit it on the frying pan and knocked the head off! So that was the end of that.

Lilly (born 1925)

While Mary was lucky enough to have the latest dolls, scooters and bicycles, children from poorer families had a lot of fun with marbles, gobs and stoppers (clay and glass bottle stoppers) or spinning tops. They sometimes made their own toys themselves:

If you couldn't pay for a ball you used to have wrapped paper, tie it up and kick a paper ball around.

Ron (born 1921)

The boys used to make scooters out of wood using a ball-bearing wheel back and front, or they'd get a box off the green-grocer – great big plank of wood and pram wheels, and they'd make a cart, and a couple would sit in the orange box and another couple would pull 'em – you had string wrapped round it.

Nellie (born 1916)

Girls, it seems, were hardly ever offered a ride in one. Ted's scooter was a 'state of the art' contraption which he had made with loving patience, skill and imagination:

When the barges come out of Surrey Docks loaded with timber, the timber was six foot high and as they clanked together some of the timber would fall in the Thames, and our job was to get a bit of timber, take it home and wait for it to dry out, and me and me friend would cut it in halves and go and get two ball bearing wheels and a block of wood and screw eyes and a bolt, and out of that we used to make a scooter!

Ted (born 1926)

He made handles and pedals for it out of wood. As a finishing touch he added a number plate:

Let's paddle. Children crowding into the paddling pool at King Edward VII Memorial Park during a heat wave in the summer of 1933. In the background is the Rotherhithe Tunnel ventilation shaft. (Copyright Getty Images)

> We used to get the milk bottle tops and put the number of our doors. As we lived in number eleven, I used to nail eleven – like two ones – making number eleven on the planks ... we'd make it strong, mind yer, and then we used to go all the way down to Greenwich on that, through the tunnel.
>
> Ted (born 1926)

This was a good four-mile round trip! Sometimes large groups of friends set off to spend the day in Greenwich on foot through the Rotherhithe tunnel, which could be entered from Shadwell Park. Parents were not worried about letting their children roam all day in this way.

People also looked back nostalgically on the happy times they spent when they were left to their own devices. 'Tin Can Copper' was a popular street game. The rules (which varied slightly from speaker to speaker) were that you had to knock down a can with a stick on it with a ball, and run around before your opponents hit you with the ball. 'High Jimmy Nacko', also called 'High Bobbery Sago' was a kind of leap-frog for boys. When the tide was out, many children went beachcombing:

> We looked for things like small clay pipes – you could find a lot of them down there as well, and if we wanted to play 'hopscotch' or something, there was always lumps of chalk, you could always go down there and get a piece of chalk and then you could mark out the hopscotch on the pavement.
>
> Bill (born 1926)

In Lizzie's family, the children entertained each other whilst their mother was out shopping:

> We'd get in our pyjamas and we'd have a quarter of apple, a quarter of orange and two palm toffees, and we'd all sit there, because they'd be up Watney Street until nine o'clock, and if it was in the winter and we had a fire, we'd sit there and tell one another ghost stories and frighten one another, you know, Saturday night, because you didn't have to go to school Sunday.
>
> Lizzie (born 1927)

Boys and girls had their separate games. Girls collected picture cards and put them in albums:

> You had a pin, a straight pin and they'd bring it down and if they come to a page where they picked one of your pictures you had to let them have the picture and they gave you the pin.
>
> Lizzie (born 1927)

George with his dogs on the
Wapping foreshore, 1925.

They also enjoyed making collections from odd ornaments, holy pictures, or coloured paper to decorate a 'grotto':

> Your mother'd give you old curtains and perhaps one of your sister's frocks that was long on yer, and you'd dress up and you'd walk along and, like, you had your grotto. You'd make a grotto on one of the loop-hole[3] things, and as the dockies come home from work, pay day, [you'd say] 'spare a penny?' and when you'd done it all you'd have a little share out of the money and that.
>
> Lizzie (born 1927)

Spinning tops and diabolos were seasonal toys, appearing in summer:

> You could spin the top and whip it – and keep whipping it, and it'd keep spinning it'd be up the road, you'd chase it, give it a whip back down again.
>
> Lilly (born 1925)

For teenagers there was not much to do in Wapping itself. Some boys joined boxing or judo clubs nearby or went out on cycling trips to Epping Forest. For younger children, the annual 'Dockers' Outing', a trip to the countryside in an open-topped bus, was unforgettable:

> We had this lovely day out at Theydon Bois with swings and music and food—oh it was absolutely lovely![4]
>
> Annie (born 1925)

> Went to the dockers' outing – they used to have outings, the Union gave my father a couple of tickets to go, that was to Theydon Bois, [laughs] when you think – the end of the world by bus! They got free tea and all cakes.
>
> Doris (born 1923)

The greatest thrill of all was, of course, the cinema. The Cable invariably heaved with noisy, excited youngsters at every showing. Before the film began, a man came round and sprayed the premises with disinfectant to keep the bugs down. There was also a comic exchange at The Cable. On Saturday mornings there were more films for children at the 'Penny Pictures' organised by the Methodist church.

At nearly ninety, Ernie looked back happily on getting up to mischief with his friends:

> … being children and playing about, we used to tie the doors with rope, each door. The people, on finding they could not open their door would shout 'constable, constable, undo the door!'
>
> Ernie (born 1913)

'Knocking down Ginger' – knocking on doors and then running away – was another favourite trick. Bill loved feeding the horses while they were waiting in the street:

> I called up to my mother for a sandwich and she thought 'Wonderful, he's eating' so she threw a sandwich wrapped in a piece of paper, and I found that the horses liked it so I gave it to the horses and called up for another sandwich.
>
> Bill (born 1926)

Most boys used to jump on the backs of vans for a ride:[5]

> In those days – cos we was always running about, running in the streets – the horses and carts used to go along there and we used to jump on the tail-board for a ride until the carman see you. 'GERRORFF!!!' he'd shout at you and you'd have to jump off.
>
> Ted (born 1926)

> Sometimes he'd sling a whip round, you know, whoever was driving it, but if the whip wasn't long enough it wouldn't catch you.
>
> Norman (born 1919)

One thing that was strictly forbidden was swimming in the river, because of the serious risks from the pollution and the tides. Naturally, many children took no notice of this:

> We was always down the river paddling up to here in the water – we never see the dangers. I'd be *terrified* if I'd have seen any of my children doing that!
>
> Lilly (born 1925)

Once Bill did fall into the river. He tried to dry off before he went home in the hope that his mother would not find out but she gave him a severe 'tongue lashing'.
Paddling in the river was somehow more appealing than the safer option of Tower Beach[6]:

> I went down to the beach, but what happened, they chucked so much sand on there, but they forgot, you get the ebb and tide, you get the tide running up and the tide running back and what happened to the sand? It just got washed away didn't it!
>
> Ted (born 1926)

Not everybody had the money for the local swimming baths,[7] a short walk out of Wapping. Norman, evidently a bit of a dare-devil, preferred swimming in the river:

> We used to creep down there [to the shore]. I've even swum through Tower Bridge, through the middle right down to Shadwell Park – that's a fair swim. It's alright with the tide, not too bad, you know. It's a bit awkward to go against the tide! Well, we always used to know what was going on, on the Thames. You knew whether there was any boats coming up. See, if the tide was low, there wouldn't be any ships coming through because they used to come up with the tide and the tide would be high very likely, and they'd be moored up before the change. There was a lot that used to swim round there [*chuckling*] – it used to be enjoyable. We used to take a bottle of lemonade and maybe a bar of chocolate and go on one of the barges. There used to be some dummy barges along there where some of the boats used to moor up for a certain time before they could moor up alongside the jetty, you know, and it used to be enjoyable summertime, nice to lay out and get the sun.
>
> Norman (born 1919)

Despite 'knocking down ginger' and other such pranks, people believed that children were far more obedient in those days. Mary's grandmother, who had worked in Queen Victoria's household, apparently used to say that:

> ... the old King that was, and the Prince of Wales, was worse than any two boys in Wapping. She said they'd climb trees in their garden, and then go asking their grandmother to mend their trousers before they went out.
>
> Mary (born 1912)

Skinny dipping at Wapping in the 1930s. (Copyright Mary Evans Picture Library)

Children generally respected their parents' rules:

> You'd go down and play in the streets 'til a certain time but as soon as your mother or your father come out and shouted out for you to go in to get ready for bed, they'd call yer, and you had to go right away.
>
> Lizzie (born 1927)

The strong network of grown-ups in authority included elders from every strand of a child's life – parents, teachers, the clergy, neighbours and relations, not to mention the police:

> The people here being such a knit community, if you sauced one of them you'd get a slap round the ear-hole, and when your Dad came up from the pub [he'd say] 'So you've been saucy again!' – and you'd get another one to straighten you up!
>
> Ted (born 1926)

> And if there was any ruins you'd climb over the ruins and you'd say 'Wait, don't go over yet, look this woman knows my Mum.' You couldn't even play truant – people would see you and they'd say 'ain't you so and so's boy?'
>
> Ron (born 1921)

> … of a night time at ten o'clock there used to be the police going on duty all in line.
>
> Ernie (born 1913)

An article in the *City and East London Observer* in 1939 refers to a couple of Wapping lads aged nineteen who were 'loitering with intent'. Although they were not charged with any offence, the magistrate announced that they would be sent to Borstal if arrested a second time:

> No-one broke a window – they wouldn't dare, because we had police patrolling the streets.
>
> Lilly (born 1925)

Everybody knew the local bobby – a certain officer number 194 was remembered as 'a right demon' and locals made up a song parodying his behaviour:

> We used to have a policeman, a bobby on a bike and if he caught you doing anything wrong he'd truly swipe you, give you a right one, you know, and you daren't go and tell our parents, daren't because you'd get another

one on top! Because he would never hit you or go for you unless you'd done something wrong. And they was always on the side of the police.

Kathleen (born 1934)

Schoolteachers regularly used corporal punishment:

The headmaster, Mr Rich used to say 'Where you bin?' 'Running errands, Sir' and he'd say 'Fiddlesticks!' and you had the cane, and you used to get one on the bottom, and you'd finish up sitting on the concrete to cool it off.

Ted (born 1926)

Children were strictly banned from pubs. The only exception to this was when a child was sent to the pub to fetch a drink for his grandmother at home:

Well, you couldn't go in a pub, but when you opened the door in the cold winter, someone would say close that door!' – all the cold air going in – but when you showed 'em the jug, the bloke would come, take the money, get a pint of ale and you'd take it back …

Ted (born 1924)

Smoking only became widespread during the Second World War, when cigarettes were part of the rations in the forces:

Good gracious, if I got caught smoking I'd have got the belt off me father!

Ted (born 1926)

Parents were forever anxious about their daughters meeting the wrong sort of man and getting into trouble:

And woe betide us, whenever any of us went out, we had to be in by ten o'clock, especially me elder sisters – and that one with the bow on her hair [pointing to a photograph], she died seven years ago, she was a villain! She loved to go out dancing, and before she went out, my Dad always used to, like, see what they were wearing – and if she had a V-neck [he would say] 'Take that frock off!' so every time she wore it out afterwards she kept her coat on the cut! [to cover the neck]

Elsie (born 1913)

Janet's father was particularly controlling:

He used to say as I was growing up – naturally your frocks get a bit shorter as you're growing up – 'Look at her!' he said 'Showing her arse!' It only used to be short above me knees! And when it came to going shopping, for some reason he didn't want me to go up the road on me own, even in daylight.

Janet (born 1921)

Childhood came to an abrupt end at fourteen when it was time to go out to work. Perhaps it was because childhood was so short that people treasured the relative freedom and security all the more.

Notes

1. The Hermitage was an area of Wapping.
2. The Cable Cinema on Cable Street.
3. A door in a warehouse through which goods were delivered by crane.
4. Near Epping Forest in Essex.
5. Vans were horse-drawn carts.
6. Tower Beach was created in 1934 to be enjoyed by children of London. Over 1,500 tons of sand were transported to the mud flat under the Tower of London.
7. The Betts Street Baths which were also used as a washhouse until 1960.

12

SCHOOL

There were five schools in Wapping of which three, St Peter's, St Patrick's and St John's Charity School, were church schools. Hermitage and Brewhouse Lane Elementary Schools[1] were run by the local authority. A few children attended schools outside Wapping, such as the prestigious Raine's in Stepney.[2] Naturally enough, in the church schools, religion was a large part of a child's life:

I think it [religion] was rammed down their throats, and I think they sort of grew up to it, and they didn't mind because it was rammed from the age of three. They started the school at three, you see they had nursery classes as well.

Barbara (teacher St Peter's School 1949)

Going to church had always been part of the school week at both St Peter's and St John's:

Every Thursday they came to school and they had to go to a service – only on Thursday, and we didn't go into lessons until about ten o'clock or something and I remember even the little ones had to be absolutely silent with their hands together, and some of the staff were watching, and if any child misbehaved at all, I remember there would be a loud whisper 'If you do that again, I'll smack your bottom!'

Barbara (teacher at St Peter's School 1949)

During the 1930s, attendance at church was dwindling.[3] The clergy tried to boost the numbers by means of a 'carrot and stick' approach:

I was at St Peter's and you used to have a little card with a stamp on it, and if you went to Mass on Sunday you got a stamp, and if you missed they wanted to know why! And you used to have to have three stamps, that's three weeks running, you'd get a ticket and you'd go up, I think it was the Co-op in Commercial Road at the time, and you'd get a pair of school shoes ... I know if you missed, they really wanted to know why, and you'd get a wallop.

Janet (born 1921)

St Patrick's school was run by nuns who left a lasting impression on many of their pupils:

I was taught by a few nuns. Sister Vincent was our headmistress and Sister Mary. Then we had a little nun, I think her name now was Sister Veronica but she used to come round and visit yer – she'd come to your Mum and all that sort of thing.

Lizzie (born 1927)

Barbara recalled the atmosphere of St Peter's School in 1949. She remembered the concrete playground, and described the classroom she taught in as 'pretty dingy':

I don't remember any windows. They must have been high up so the children couldn't look out – that's usually the thing – to avoid children's minds wandering and because there was a lot going on in the docks round about.

Barbara (teacher at St Peter's School 1949)

Rest time for the children, St Peter's London Docks, Infant School.

St Patrick's School, 1927. Note the nun in her elaborate headdresses. Doris is in the top row, second right.

She described her fellow teachers as 'a bit stiff and starchy' but she felt that they were committed to their vocation.

Founded in 1695 for the poor children of the parish, the charity school of St John of Wapping was the oldest of all the schools. The elegant building, with its statue of a boy and a girl above the two entrances on either side of the façade, dates back to 1760. In the early years of the twentieth century, St John of Wapping School aimed to prepare children for respectable jobs. The most successful boys obtained apprenticeships, and the top girls became domestic servants. The school rules laid great emphasis on cleanliness and regular attendance at church. In 1931, according to the school log book, the curriculum consisted of: arithmetic, English grammar, reading, penmanship, drawing, general business correspondence, music and singing, senior drill, geography, nature study, needlework, spelling, literature, composition, New Testament, history, catechism and prayer books (for seniors, juniors and infants).

The aim of elementary schools was to enable all working-class children to learn 'the three Rs'. However, not everybody, by any means, left school being able to read and write. Lilly implied that she was the only member of her family who could:

> My brother never heard from us – he was out in Egypt, you know, with Montgomery and I was the only one who used to write to him cos I was the only one that had any [education].
>
> Lilly (born 1925)

Teachers laid great emphasis on practising good handwriting. George, who attended Brewhouse Lane School, had a soft spot for his teacher who taught him how to write in beautiful copperplate. Children learned by rote with, according to Barbara, very little opportunity to think for themselves. She was impressed and moved by the imagination of her pupils when they were given a chance to develop their own ideas for a change:

May Day celebrations.

I brought them all along to school one Friday afternoon and I said 'Lets make the London Docks'. And they had all sorts of ideas I'd never have thought of, and they made barges, and they made lighters – of course their fathers were working in the London Docks and they knew exactly what to do. They made lovely things.

Barbara (teacher at St Peter's School 1949)

Housewifery was a subject that girls were expected to take seriously. What a woman needed to know above everything else was how run the home. In those days there was a lot more to housework than there is today. Grace Foakes describes the complexities of laundering which she learnt at housewifery school: she was taught the correct way to wash clothes, and how to use three different sorts of iron: a flat iron, a goffering iron (a narrow iron with a pointed end which was used to press pleats into a frill) and a smoothing iron.[4] She was also taught how to starch clothes properly. Lizzie remembered being released from St Patrick's to go to a school of housewifery for one day per week:

You used to learn how to do all things to do with the house, like – but one week I took me Dad's bowler hat to clean it out.

Lizzie (born 1927)

Since all men wore bowler hats, a girl had to learn how to steam them and make them shine. Peggy remembered coming under the teacher's scrutiny when she inspected the girls' work at the end of the housewifery class:

You dusted or you made the beds, and she'd come round and go *like that*, and see if there was any dust – wonderful! This is what's been lost – I find this is what a lot of children have lost, it may sound a bit old fashioned, but it give you something, showed you the way to do it. Ironing, oh yes oh yes, you had to do ironing. You could take your own things sometimes – you could wash them and dry them and then you'd iron them and take them home. Or you could make cakes and things and then you took them home.

Peggy (born 1920)

Empire Day, Brewhouse Lane School, *c.*1929. (Copyright Tower Hamlets Local History Library)

The highlight of the school year was the annual religious procession, for which there was always much preparation and excitement. St Patrick's also organised a lot of fundraising concerts and other special events to pay back the large debt incurred when their new school building was opened in 1935.

St John's School organised regular outings and treats for the children: they were taken to see the Lord Mayor's Show, or taken out to Greenwich for the day and given buns and two new pennies. Every child was invited to the end of term party where, if they were lucky, they could win oranges and sweets as prizes. Although charity was well meant, not everybody appreciated it:

> Every Christmas we used to get a pair of boots and I used to *hate* that – a pair of boots and a pair of black stockings and two new pennies.
>
> Nellie (born 1916)

She hated the boots 'because it wasn't the fashion, was it! ... but you *had* to wear them, you know'.

The King's birthday was a school holiday, just as it was for the dock workers. On Empire Day, the children took part in a traditional service full of rousing patriotic sentiments.[5]

Empire Day service 1932[6]

Hymn	O God our Help in Ages Past.
Prayers	For the King and Empire
Special song	The Garden of Britain
Song	Britannia! The Pride of the Ocean!
Song	The Union Jack
Solo	Among our Ancient Mountains
Address	Our Glorious Empire
Procession	Flags and march past
The Salute and special song	The Flag of Britain (with unfolding of the Union Jack)
God Save the King	
Dismissal	

Teachers tended to be authoritarian:

> My teacher was Miss Casey and she used to play the fiddle, and I don't know how many times I got a wallop on top of the head with the fiddle! [*laughs*]. And they used to do horrible things to you, like they sat us in the middle of the floor once with the bottom half off my Charlie [her brother] and made him hold a daffodil, cos he pulled all the daffodils and he shouldn't have done ... it was alright, it was good they were strict, you know.
>
> Kathleen (born 1934)

Norman was always getting into trouble:

> I got punished alright – you used to get the cane if you was late. I got that plenty of times – across there [*showing the back of his hand*].

He reflected that it 'wasn't bad', and agreed with his wife, Sal when she said:

> It didn't hurt us really because you respected people, didn't yer.
>
> Norman (born 1919), Sal (born 1925)

St Peter's had stopped corporal punishment by the time Barbara was there in 1949:

> There had been caning before I came because there was this story that I heard that the children who had misbehaved had lined up. First of all they had to kneel on the hard board floor, which is very painful, for quite a long time if they behaved badly, and then they used to line up and get whacked on the hand with a ruler – not very hard.
>
> Barbara (teacher at St Peter's School 1949)

Several people had positive things to say about their school days. George thought that he had received a good grounding, both at his infant school and his junior school. Perhaps he was biased because he met his sweetheart at junior school and they enjoyed a long marriage.

Children who were evacuated during the war inevitably had to cope with a lot of disruption to their schooling. During the War, St Peter's moved to Brighton and St Patrick's moved to Guildford. Ted was one of a few children who stayed behind in Wapping:

> And one of the teachers, Mr Farrell, he never went – they all went to, I don't know, Guildford, that way out – and he stayed here, and he went into Jackman House, [to] a woman by name of Mrs Clark. There were six of us, and he used to teach us round a table.
>
> Ted (born 1926)

Bill had a particularly unsettling time during the War, when he had to change schools several times:

> Every time you moved, you went to a school and it was back to square one, you know, one and one makes… C A T spells 'cat' and that's the way it started. That's why I never got any higher.
>
> Bill (born 1926)

In 1932 St Peter's School had 400 children. After the War and the baby boom that followed it, the numbers increased dramatically:

> I was given this huge class of seventy children after the post-war bulge and I was given the six and seven year olds, and we had to have them reading by the time they were seven 'or else'. And of course this was almost impossible.
>
> Barbara (1949)

Most people expected to leave school at fourteen:

> When you got to be fourteen you went to work, I mean further education wasn't part of our lifestyle even though my father and mother were intelligent people.
>
> Annie (born 1925)

Ted admitted that he did not have any ambition:

> I was very clever the other way [i.e. at truanting], but as long as you could do 'the three Rs' you could get by.
>
> Ted (born 1926)

Looking back, Norman realised that in different circumstances he might have gone to art school:

> I didn't like school at all. I went to three schools, infants and then infants up to eleven and then from eleven, I went along Wapping High Street to the Hermitage. The only thing I was interested in at school was drawing…and I was the second best in the school … and I've always liked drawing, and me Dad used to look over me shoulder sometimes, and I never got any help, and he said 'Oh, that's good!' and that was it. They all recognised it but it didn't make no difference – them days, they didn't care… nobody bothered, not even me Dad.
>
> Norman (born 1919)

Both Doris and Lilly won scholarships to a secondary school in Stepney after passing an entrance examination. For Doris, this was a passport to a good job as a solicitor's secretary in the City. Lilly suffered from a lack of self-confidence and could not settle at her new school:

> When I was eleven or twelve, I'm not sure which, twelve I think it was, we used to do a scholarship. We had one nun there, she encouraged me, she must have known I had the potential … Sister Louise. Well I got through the scholarship, and I had to go to St Bernard's then … well I never liked it. I think it was because I felt inferior. A lot of them were snobbish girls, you know what kids are. A lot of them come from over New Cross

and that way. They were very, very snobbish ... so I turned it in, come back to St Patrick's. Then War started, so probably with the War and all I probably would never have gone traipsing up to there every morning.

Lilly (born 1925)

Reflecting on this, she realised that, had she stayed at St Bernard's, she might have been able to go to college or university.

Although some of the people interviewed had not been given the chance to reach their potential, many of them would later take great pride in the achievements of their children.

Notes

1. Elementary education was introduced in 1870, making school attendance compulsory for all children.
2. Henry Raine (1679-1738) was a philanthropist who made his money in brewing. The school provided places for fifty boys and fifty girls. The school was founded in 1719 in Wapping where the original building still stands.
3. According to the school log book of St John's, in August 1931, 40 per cent of the children were not attending church or catechism class on Sundays.
4. *My Part of the River*, Grace Foakes
5. Empire Day, 24 May was renamed 'Commonwealth Day 'in 1958.
6. Empire Day Service source, St John's Charity School log book.

13

CHURCH

Built in the eighteenth century, St John of Wapping was the oldest of the three churches.[1] It was bombed during the War, leaving only the tower intact. St Patrick's Church was founded by Cardinal Manning in 1877, and St Peter's London Docks, a High Anglican church using 'smells and bells', was founded by Charles Lowder in 1856. Both these men were figures of national importance, who connected this obscure part of London with the mainstream of British life. There was also Benn's Chapel[2], a congregational meeting house, and small communities of Catholic and Protestant nuns.

There have been many philanthropic clergymen in Wapping over the last 150 years. Some of them have been commemorated in streets and council blocks.[3] An outstanding example was Lincoln Stanhope Wainwright, Vicar of St Peter's, London Docks from 1874 to 1929, who has been described as a modern St Francis of Assisi. Many people remembered his kindness and charity when they were children and in need.

Father Wainwright established a club twinning Wapping boys with the boys of Radley College public school in Oxfordshire. Frank visited Radley College with St Peter's Boys' Club when he was a teenager in the thirties. He had marvelled at the facilities available to Radley boys: a swimming pool in the school grounds, and their *own study* with personal tea and coffee-making facilities! He remembered an occasion when members of the Radley College came to Wapping for a boxing match. As he was getting ready for the fight (the proud owner of black boxer shorts with his initials in red piping, made by his sister-in-law), a man wearing a bowler hat with *The Times* tucked under his arm asked him if he was fighting his son. He said 'yes' and the man said 'Give him a good thrashing – I caught him smoking a woodbine!' Frank won the match and the boy's father came up to congratulate him, pressing half a crown into his hand.[4]

According to Lucy Menzies, Father Wainwright's funeral in 1929 was a momentous event in Wapping. Hundreds of sailors, dockers and shopkeepers lined the streets, their caps doffed, and crowds of women and children came out to watch the funeral procession go by. All the blinds were drawn, women made special wreaths for the occasion and children laid violets on the coffin. Other churchmen succeeding Father Wainwright also had a loyal following.

The influence of the clergy extended far beyond the church. Not only did they run most of the schools, but they also were very involved with what went on in the hospital. Members of the clergy had intimate knowledge of families they visited regularly in their homes, especially in times of trouble, and people were well used to the sight of the vicar or priest on the street, as he walked by in his cassock. Nuns, also conspicuous because of their elaborate headdress and habit, were out and about and did a good deal of pastoral work. Doris commented that she missed seeing the nuns in their habits:

> We got nuns now. You wouldn't know they were nuns, would you? I don't know whether it's for the good or the bad – because they're out in their Marks and Spencer trousers, you don't know who they are.
>
> Doris (born 1923)

Ada remembered being ill at home with scarlet fever when she was a child:

> There was a sister at St John's Church who used to come home to me; she was very, very nice and I think she was a nurse in her own rights and she used to see to me.
>
> Ada (born 1909)

Above left: St John's Church, 1936.
(Copyright Tower Hamlets Local History
Library)

Above right: Father Wainwright preaching.
In 1873, when Father Wainwright first
arrived in Wapping, drunkenness and
prostitution were rife. Initially people
were very hostile to him and Irish
Catholics threw stones at him when he
walked about the streets preaching on
Good Friday. He devoted his entire life
to the poor and needy and soon hostility
was replaced by love and respect.

Right: Father Pollock's funeral, 1939.
Father Pollock came to Wapping in 1893
and remained there until his death. When
he died, 'hundreds of Wapping people
stood outside St Peter's Church when
the news broke of his death and many
shops covered their windows with black
boards.' (*City and East London Observer*,
May 1939. Every attempt for obtaining
permission to reproduce this photograph
has been made)

Church of England Temperance Society. Children dressed in their Sunday best, girls in white dresses and lace caps, boys in sailor suits parading banners for local temperance societies. The large banner in the middle of the photograph reads: 'Church of England Temperance Society, Stepney Deanery, Ruridecanal Juvenile Union, Junior Band of Hope, Challenge Banner, For General Efficiency.'

Lilly was a little afraid of the priest when she was girl:

> We held them in awe because if you ever saw them go along with their hand in their coat, they used to have the sacrament where they'd be going round to St George's hospital or going home to someone who was dying. You never, ever looked at them cos it was more or less forbidden.
>
> Lilly (born 1925)

Charitable events organised by the churches played an important part in people's social lives. There were the Christmas parties for poor children, the St Peter's Church holiday camps, community parties (to celebrate national events such as coronations), not to mention numerous clubs for people of all ages. In the thirties, for example, St Patrick's Church ran a mother's guild, a sewing guild, a young women's drama club and frequent fundraising dances. Elsie made the most of the St Peter's Church clubs when she was growing up in the twenties:

> I used to go to St Peter's club, singing classes, keep fit, Band of Hope.
>
> Elsie (born 1913)

The Band of Hope was a national temperance organisation for children founded in 1847.[5] Apart from the activities organised by the churches there was not much for young people to do in Wapping:

> We used to go gym, tap dancing things like that – St Patrick's of an evening ... and that was somewhere to go.
>
> Doris (born 1923)

People were allowed to join the church clubs on condition they attended church regularly. Bill used to enjoy meeting his friends at St John's Church Club:

> But one day the vicar said 'Well you're supposed to come to church because this is a church club and most of you lot don't come to church so I'm going to close the club' – so he closed the club.
>
> Bill (born 1926)

The spirit of evangelism in Wapping was still very much alive in the twenties and thirties. Grace Foakes had witnessed open-air services during her childhood around 1910 when hymn books were handed out in the streets and people were accompanied by a harmonium on Sundays. Father Wainwright continued this tradition preaching from a portable pulpit in the docks. Lilly, who was a Catholic, remembered that the vicar from St Peter's came to preach in her street in the thirties:

> On Good Friday there used to be a – they used to call it, 'the meat wagon' –it used to come round with, like, a pulpit on a barrow on wheels. Father Pollock, from St Peter's – he used to give a Good Friday sermon and you'd used to hear one having a laugh at them and them having a laugh at the Pope.

Belonging to a church was an important part of a person's identity as someone from Wapping. People who lived 'over the bridge' belonged to St George in the East, a different parish. Protestants talked about being 'brought up at St Peter's and Catholics felt similarly:

> I had to go to church – St Patrick's – otherwise you couldn't make your communion, couldn't walk in the processions and all that.
>
> Kathleen (born 1934)

In the thirties there were services at all times of day on a Sunday to suit everybody:

> My Mum used to get up and go to Mass, Sunday eight o'clock, and someone used to have her breakfast ready time for when she used to come back … and then we always used to go ten o'clock Mass cos it was the children's Mass and me brothers and sisters who went to work, if they had a bit of a lay-in, they went twelve o'clock Mass, but people all went to Church, didn't they.
>
> Lizzie (born 1927)

In 1913 there were as many as seven Sunday services at St Peter's. You stood out if you did not belong to a local church. Lilly realised that she had been excluded from St Patrick's and shunned by other Catholics because she was illegitimate:

> I've got a feeling, I don't know … why was I christened up in St Mary's and Michael's when I lived round the corner?[6] I've got a feeling the priest wouldn't christen me. And my godmother was a Protestant. I don't think nobody else would stand godmother for me and that was in St Mary's and St Michael's.
>
> Lilly (born 1925)

The high points in the church year and for the community were the church processions. Catholics throughout the East End and beyond celebrated the second Sunday in May, Corpus Christi, in accordance with a long tradition going back to the Middle Ages. A May Queen selected from St Patrick's School by one of the teachers carried the statue of the Virgin decorated with lilies through the streets of Wapping, followed by the procession of beautifully dressed children. This was the one day in the year when Wapping was open to the rest of the world:

> You had people coming from miles around – you had aunts and uncles you'd never even heard of!
>
> Ted (born 1926)

> That was one day for everybody who had moved out of Wapping to come back, and the streets used to be full and there'd be altars and flowers in every turning. Oh, it was really beautiful! The men used to come out and whitewash the walls, and pretty altars, and down the bottom there, Reardon Street, used to be a really beautiful altar, [the] biggest one there.
>
> Kathleen (born 1934)

The priest led the procession which wound slowly through the streets bright with flags and bunting, accompanied by the St Patrick's Church traditional Irish drum and fife band.[7] Every few yards he would stop to bless the home-made altars people had created by removing their window frames and covering tables outside and inside with a white sheet:

St Peter's Day procession. The banner reads, 'Sancta Maria, ora pro nobis'.

The band used to come out to bless the altars, and all the people, all the kids and the people would follow Father Reardon or Cannon Reardon and they'd stand near [the altars] and they'd sing a hymn and they'd go round to the next one and that would go right round 'til nine o'clock and they'd come back and then they'd all assemble outside the church near the park, and the band used to play "God bless our Pope" and you'd all stand there singing ... People used to all stand round the kerbs and watch and when the procession was over you came and had your tea – you had a right slap up tea, you know.

Lizzie (born 1927)

The day was sometimes referred to as 'Salad Sunday' or 'Cucumber Sunday' because of the tradition of having salad for tea. Afterwards people sang Irish songs and listened to the band playing Irish jigs in the pubs until the small hours:

You used to get processions from the Catholic church every year, once a year and everybody looked forward to it – we all used to watch it, Catholics and Protestants, didn't make no difference.

Norman (born 1919)

Preparations for the great day started months in advance. All the children at St Patrick's School took part in the procession and girls had immaculate white dresses especially for the occasion. Doris' came from a Jewish tailor:

My mother bought all my procession dresses from Cohen's up in Watney, [market] you know.

Doris (born 1923)

Annie, whose family were Protestants, had reservations about Procession Day:

But these children were very, very poor and most of the fathers worked in the docks, and nine times out of ten they couldn't get a day's work. But when it was the Catholic procession they all had – and this has always puzzled me – they all had the most loveliest dresses and white shoes and white socks and little veils on their head…well it was much like what goes on in Ireland …the Church is pretty dominant and I'm not sure that it's a very good idea really.

Annie (born 1925)

In his account of the Catholic processions of his day, Patrick Hanshaw describes how parents would sometimes run up debts in order to buy the right clothing for the event, rather than let the side down.[8] St Peter's Church had its own procession day at Petertide, 29 June, which had been going ever since Father Lowder initiated it 1873.

Most people appreciated the good works of the clergy and many, like Doris, also must have felt that they stood up for ordinary members of the community in political matters:

In the past we had priests what were fighters.

Doris (born 1923)

In turn the people were expected to support the Church. Catholic priests visited families regularly to ask for money:

We used to have one priest we used to have down there, and he always used to come home and visit yer – like everyday, to get his money. You had to pay him money. It was only like two pence, that's all – and he'd go round every house, bless the house and get his two pence or whatever – if you wanted to give him more you give it to him.

Kathleen (born 1934)

Recalling the priest's visits for money made Lilly feel resentful. As far as she was concerned, the priest was no different from the tally man or the coal man who also came to collect money on a Sunday:

Altar for Procession Sunday. The sign in front of the altar reads 'St Patrick's Repair Fund'.

When I think of it, every Sunday the priest used to come round for chapel money. Now, my mother had three children to keep and she worked in the hospital, and the priest used to come round for money. I find that bitter. And not only that, he used to have the chapel boy with him who used to take the money – *he* never took it. I think it was about sixpence – that was a lot of money when you only earned £2s 5d per week.

Lilly (born 1925)

The priest, on the other hand was enjoying a life of comparative luxury:

That door [the clergy house] was never open. And he used to have a housekeeper as well. And you used to have two of them there – there was always two priests, so they had to be *kept*.

Lilly (born 1925)

Much of the money collected was used as 'brick money' to build St Patrick's School. The topic of 'outdoor collections' crops up frequently in the St Patrick's Church notice book. One entry reads:

Thanks to those who so generously subscribed to Cannon Reardon's robe fund. He would be grateful to receive offerings from any that have not yet given.

Kathleen was on very friendly terms with the priest:

One day again, something dropped off the back of a lorry. It was all tinned pears, and a crowd of us had quite a few tins as it happened, so he's sitting there, so I've got a load of them on the table, haven't I, and some custard for the kids, and he said 'Oh, they look nice!' so I said 'Oh, you can have some' I said 'as a matter of fact, you can take a couple of tins, cos I got them for nothing.' So I said 'I tell you, Father, they dropped off the back of a lorry.' He said 'never mind, my dear' he said 'I'll go back and I'll confess!' It was so funny, it was; we used to have some laughs, really good laughs.

Kathleen (born 1934)

Annie was invited by the Catholic priest to join his school:

I do recall going to school once, and we saw the Catholic priest. My sister and I were walking along together and he stopped us … he said 'Where do you go to school, children?' – so we told him, so he said, 'Would you like to come to my school?' So I said, 'Well, you would have to ask my mother' but when I told my mother, she was absolutely furious because we weren't Catholics anyway, and she was going to see him and tell him off … I think he quite liked – cos my mother kept us very nice – like a lot of the kids weren't kept very nice and I'm not saying that's bad or right, but I'm just saying that that's perhaps the way it was, and I think he quite liked these two neat little children and nicely mannered, because my mother was very fussy about that, and he probably would have liked us to have gone to his school, St Patrick's, but he had a bit of a cheek to say that, didn't he!

Annie (born 1925)

There was very little real friction between the two religious communities. People from different faiths were on friendly terms and mixed socially too. The clergy also worked together sometimes – Father Reardon and Father Wainwright were apparently the best of friends and were often seen visiting the Infirmary together.[9] According to Madge Darby, Protestants drew the line at the London County Council's proposal to change the name of 'Old Gravel Lane' to 'Cardinal Pole Street'.[10] In the end the LCC settled on the name 'Wapping Lane'.

School children took the rivalry between Catholics and Protestants a little more to heart. Catholics called the Protestants, 'Proddydogs':

[On] St Patrick's Day we used to come and pinch their ribbon and they used to come and pinch our red, white and blue ribbon – always squabbles over it – we never really got on well, St Patrick's and St Peter's 'til after the war.[11]

Elsie (born 1913)

There were certain boundaries between the two communities which people knew they should never overstep:

> You'd be *banished* if you went to St Peter's Church when I was a kid – it was taboo!
>
> Lilly (born 1925)

Inevitably some young men and women belonging to different churches fell in love:

> Up to about twenty, I went to St Peter's Church, and, course, I started courting a Catholic girl and they couldn't get over it – fighting and all that – oh! cos I done everything at St Peter's, I done everything for them, and to think I could get married to a Catholic – oh, that was dreadful.
>
> Eric (born 1913)

The Church exerted power and influence on the whole community. As an outsider who had worked in other parts of the East End, Pam was struck by how 'respectable' Wapping seemed in comparison. The relatively peaceful atmosphere of Wapping was a 'different world' from the streets of Stepney where there were prostitutes, alcoholics and homeless people at large. She attributed this partly to the settled nature of the community, but also felt that the Church maintained law and order. Barbara thought along similar lines:

> You didn't hear any lurid stories of anyone being set upon or anything. And I think the churches had something to do with it. You see, the priests were walking about everywhere with their cassocks on, and the Sisters were always around. I think there was a sort of benevolent feeling that everybody was looking after everybody else.
>
> Barbara (teacher at St Peter's School 1949)

Jack put it this way:

> Down Wapping, if you got any trouble you called the priest, not a policeman. There was always trouble Saturday, always trouble Friday and Saturday night with drink with the police, but then you didn't call the police, you called the priest, then he would come and would say 'Mr O 'Flynn, come out!'
>
> Jack (born 1924)

Notes

1. St John's Church of Wapping was first built in 1617, then demolished and rebuilt in 1760.
2. London Congregational Evangelistic Association, part of the East London Mission, and founded by John Benn. Several members of the Benn family became prominent politicians including two MPs for Wapping. The long line of politicians has continued with Tony and Hilary Benn.
3. For example Lowder House, Wainwright House, Reardon Street.
4. In today's money 12½p.
5. Grace Foakes mentions the Band of Hope Society for adults in Wapping in her time. Women who joined the society were given a brooch in the shape of a white bow to signify that they were teetotal.
6. A church in Stepney.
7. There were also bagpipes.
8. *All My Yesterdays*, Patrick Hanshaw.
9. Jack Banfield, transcript, Museum in Docklands.
10. Madge Darby, *Tender Grace*, vol. V.
11. Catholics wore green ribbons.

14

LEISURE

In general, people had very little leisure and couples spent still less time together. Women were hard at work with their chores most of the time, sparing a few moments to chat to their neighbours on their front steps while most men worked Monday to Saturday. While some better-off families had holidays at the seaside or in country hotels, poorer families mostly had working holidays:

> I've never had a holiday in my life. My children certainly made up for it. The only holiday they ever got was when we used to go fruit picking. And they loved it. Picked strawberries. They used to pick their own and they kept their own money, and then Saturday afternoon, they'd have a good splash out.
>
> Lilly (born 1925)

Some families saved up a few pennies per week to put into the Country Holiday Fund to enable their children to stay in the countryside for a week or two:

> We used to pay three pence a week to go to Whitstable for a fortnight and we were in a house with twelve girls – right church people they was. Well, you can imagine us. About four slept in a bed and I don't think they got a lot. I think they got about four to five shillings a week to look after us and we were staying with them most of the time, and when you're from London a lot of people don't want to know you, especially down there.
>
> Jack (born 1924)

The hop-picking season usually lasted for three weeks, and often continued until after the beginning of the autumn term, when teachers would return to find a much depleted classroom. Nearly all the hop-picking work was done by women who stayed on the farms in Kent with their children in places such as Goudhurst, Wartingbury and Yalding. Fathers generally carried on with their jobs during the week and came down to join the family at weekends:

> When they used to go up, they'd pack their old hopping boxes, a couple of tea chests and bundles [in the] back of an old lorry and away they went!
>
> Victor (born 1930)

> The hopping lorry would go down Wapping, and me and my wife, we had to walk me mother all the way down with a couple of pails and brooms and pick the lorry up at about two o'clock in the morning because the bloke had to be at work at seven ... and about ten of us would get on the hopping lorry.
>
> Jack (born 1924)

People packed everything they needed for their stay into tea chests, prams and unwieldy bundles. Since there was no electricity, they took their own oil lamps, as well as pillows and plenty of blankets for the cool autumn nights:

> I remember all the huts and I remember when you used to have to go down there before the hopping started, because yous all used to stuff the mattresses with straw.
>
> Angie (born c. 1945), daughter of Ethel

St Peter's Church Cycling Club at Bognor, c. 1930.

In September they used to run a train from London Bridge, the hop-pickers' train, six o'clock in the morning, and all the people'd be there with their prams and pots and pans on it. We used to go to Marden and the farm would have a big wagon.

Ted (born 1926)

The farmer would meet them, load up all the luggage and take them to their temporary abode, a corrugated-iron hut which they tried to make as cosy as possible – a home from home:

You'd get a couple of [rolls of] odd wall paper for a pound ... make it look nice and you had your tea chest in there and tables and you cooked outside.

Jack (born 1924)

Before the Second World War, living conditions were very basic:

Outside tin huts with dunnies – holes in the ground and you had to walk about two hundred yards to get a pail of water, and you had faggots to make fires with to cook meals on.

Jack (born 1924)

The farmer supplied the faggots and some coke for the fires, and also allowed hoppers to use a cookhouse if the weather was bad. On fine evenings, people would cook and eat in the open, and then chat and sing around the campfire:

I can still smell the fires at night being lit ... I remember, as a child, being in a hut, being put to bed, and there used to be the crackling of the fire, and we used to lie in bed and I'd hear it spitting and there was all the stories as you was sitting round the fire.

Angie (born c. 1945), daughter of Ethel

Nellie's family in front of their hop-picking hut, Horsmonden, Kent.

Every year there was the same people, you got to know them, you know it was just like speaking to friends at the finish.

Ted (born 1926)

You used to have to get up at about five o'clock in the morning and it was cold, but once the sun came out it was lovely, you know. You used to pull them old bines down and they used to drown yer!

Norman (born 1919)

According to an edition of the *City and East London Observer* of 1939, the women and children earned between £10 and £15 during their three-weeks' hop picking. The men spent much of their time at the weekend enjoying the end-product of these labours in the pubs.

There were several processes involved in the cultivation and harvesting of hops. Ted and his family went to the hop fields when the hops were just starting to grow:

It was the start of the War – we'd go there fruit picking and me sisters and me mother would stay on and do the hop twiddling.

Ted (born 1926)

He went on to explain what was involved in 'hop twiddling':

The hops, when they'd start to grow, they'd have the strings and they'd have to trick them round the strings slowly to make sure they grew up.

I used to love the summer, but not hop-picking because as you picked the hops you got like a stain on your finger, and when you tried to eat anything it was terrible bitter!

Ted (born 1926)

Many women allowed their children to go off and play for hours on end in the countryside, fishing and scrumping whilst they carried on working:

I enjoyed it as a kid, yes, well it was different from the town: you'd go off, and no fears of anybody molesting you.

Tom (born 1923)

Jack, who spent his childhood holidays in Goudhurst every year with his mother and sisters, was expected to work:

I used to go pole pulling down there. When you're picking the hops, they pull the hop bines down – it's the parts left up the top. And you got a big pile and you'd get them down…then you have to move the bins,' fourteen bins to another patch. You're what you call a 'pole puller' and when the measurer comes out you hold the sack up, he puts the hops in.

Jack (born 1924)

Grace hated the whole experience:

They took me when I was twelve, and we went in a lorry and bandied along to Kent. We all got settled in, filling up the mattresses with straw. It used to stick in you and you'd look round and see all the cobwebs and things, and you'd get settled in this bed of a night. We'd all be crammed together 'til she went and got another hut from the farmer, you know. And then we got up – all the wet dew, all misty and cold, and put another coat on, push your boots on and that; you'd have a mug of tea and you'd have your breakfast. Then we'd get on the field, you know, and we'd get to this big bin and she'd say: 'You stand there, you pull them hops out and you pick 'em as fast as you can.' I used to say: 'Alright then', cos I was a bit dopey, and cos I was spoilt, you see. And I'd take this bine down and all the wet used to come on you like that, you know, and then you'd throw it over like that, and I'd got in the knack of picking them and then me back started to ache with one thing and another – 'Hey, you'd better do better than that, you know!' Then the man used to come and measure them and take them away, and then another empty bin would be put in its place and I'd go on 'til about one o'clock and then you'd break for a mug of tea and some bread and marge, or something like that. And then, when it come to five o'clock – and cos you used to have to run and spend a penny down in amongst the vines that hadn't been picked, and your hands used to be thick with this green stuff, it would be hurting, you know, and your back would be aching and one thing and another, and then this sound used to go on 'Pull no more bines!' 'Oh, what's this happening?' 'That's it, you're finished, now roll that, and peg it down' and 'do this' and 'do that and then we'd all walk back – it was only about a mile, and then the fires would be lit with the big bundles of wood, and all the pots used to go on, and then you'd have a lump of this pudding that they'd brought with them…and you'd eat that, you know, and then you was free to do what you liked for a while. But I hated it – *I hated it* – hhuh! But anyway the grown-ups came down weekends, they come down by train and 'How are you getting on then, Grace Emily White, are you alright?' I said 'No, I don't like it here, I wanna go home!' And so they said 'When you go back, take her with yer!' And when I got back I said 'Oh, Mum, never let me go down there no more!' 'But not the nice countryside picking up all those hazelnuts and things like that?' I said 'No, don't like it, I want to be home!'

Grace (born 1921)

For most people however, recalling hop-picking days brought back intensely happy memories of closeness within the family in a carefree setting close to nature. They 'forgot about the hard bits' when 'your tea was cooking on the fire and you would sit around it in one big happy family'.

As Jack put it:

If you had a bit of sunshine it was the highway to heaven.

Jack (born 1924)

For many people, the only other escape from the city was the annual 'beano' organised by their local pub. This was just a day trip, sponsored by the publican as a treat for his customers. From the publican's point of view it was a way of holding the customers together, encouraging their loyalty to the pub. There were separate outings for men and women. The publican hired a char-a-banc to take thirty ladies or men out to places such as Whitstable or Hastings, Margate or Ramsgate, stopping for lunch at a hotel on the way. The ladies got dressed up to the nines and clambered into the charabanc which was already loaded

Children in front of a coach setting off for a beano, 1948. The men are getting seated in the coach in front of the Jolly Sailor pub, and children are posing with their hands outstretched to catch the coins thrown to them as the coach drives off.

with Guinness and plenty of ham. As they set off, they threw coins at the groups of children standing on the kerb waiting to fight over the money, cheering and waving:

> You used to save all your pennies and ha' pennies up and all the kids used to come before you were going out and you'd throw all your money – all your pennies and two pences [sic] out the window.
>
> Lizzie (born 1927)

When the ladies arrived back in Wapping in the evening, they carried on singing as they unloaded the charabanc and returned to the pub for a few more drinks. They went on talking about the outing for weeks on end. Then it was the men's turn. After an exuberant day's drinking, the men returned the worse the wear (some of them allegedly, using their bowler hats to relieve themselves) These annual beanos occurred less and less frequently after the Second World War because of the expense.

Most dockers frequented the pub everyday after work and also at weekends. On the whole, pubs were male territory. If a woman went into a pub at all she would use the saloon bar rather than the public bar. Facilities were generally very basic and in some of the pubs there were no women's toilets. At the Jolly Sailor, one of Wapping's most popular pubs, there was just a urinal outside in a disgusting state. There was hosepipe in the door to wash the place down and tar on the walls to protect them from the urine. Women visiting the popular White Swan and Cuckoo in the 1920s resorted to relieving themselves in the courtyard, which stank. They were probably unaware of the little boys spying on them. Many women preferred to have a drink at home. They would send a child round to the pub for them:

Men chatting as they stand on Wapping Old Stairs, 1940. They may have just come out of the Town of Ramsgate pub. Note the soldiers in the background. (Copyright Getty Images)

This old person that lived in Frobisher House, old Mrs Parker, she'd have a shawl and a black cap and she used to say to us – give us a jug, earthenware jug 'Will you go to The Star and get us a pint of ale?' And she had a poker in the fire; she used to knock it and put the poker into her ale to warm it up.

Ted (born 1926)

Ethel remembered her mother's favourite drink:

Half a bottle of beer and a pint of lemonade, put the poker in the fire, red hot the poker, in goes the lemonade and it all frothed up.

Ethel (born 1916)

Gambling was popular, which caused much concern amongst the clergy. Since this was illegal, people had to be on their guard to avoid discovery by the police, especially if they played cards outdoors:

My Nan used to sit at the window, you know. Of a day they used to sit in the square down there and play cards for money – dice and that – and my Nan used to always watch, cos if the police came along, she'd throw out a cup of water over 'em to let them know the police was coming.

Kathleen (born 1934)

Some people had fond memories of family parties at home, reminiscing nostalgically about singing old favourites around the piano or accordion, or playing cards all evening for ha' pennies and pennies:

And if you had a party, you all had to get up and do a turn – you all had to get up and sing whether you had a good voice or you didn't have a good voice, and everyone 'ould join and you'd get up and do a little knees-up.

Lizzie (born 1927)

Lilly was not so fortunate:

> Well they never had the rooms for celebrations then, they was little tenements.
>
> Lilly (born 1925).

At New Year, however, there was a street party for everybody:

> On New Year's night, we used to have the Scotch boats coming in to the Hermitage Wharf. All the young girls used to go after the sailors, the Scotch sailors, and New Year's night, they used to light a great big bonfire on that bridge, didn't they ... and the Wapping people used to go and drink in the Scotch Arms and the China [Ship].
>
> Lizzie (born 1927)

> They used to bring the piano down into the street and aw! there used to be crowds all singing and dancing.
>
> Nellie (born 1916)

Elsie's parents took all their children to shows in the West End:

> We used to go up the Stoll Theatre – next to the Lyceum, my Mum and Dad always used to take us to the Pantomime ... that was a shilling up right up in the gods. They used to go to a pub round the corner and us kids was looking after our place until we started moving, somebody said 'Quick go and get Mum and Dad, quick, we won't get in!'
>
> Elsie (born 1913)

A night at the pictures was an alternative to going to the pub although Wapping itself did not have a cinema:

> It used to be nice going to the cinema those days, cos when Hitler used to come up there'd be all booing and everything!
>
> Elsie (born 1913)

Of all the many cinemas nearby, perhaps the most popular was the Troxy[2] which opened in 1933 with the film *King Kong*. This was a lavish people's palace, with thick carpets, floor-to-ceiling mirrors and chandeliers. The Wurlitzer organ was an added attraction and an object of fascination as it rose from under the stage.

Notes

1. Bins were large sacking bags supported by poles.
2. On the corner of Commercial Road and Pitsea Street, now a bingo hall.

15

JEWS

Only a few yards beyond Wapping in Shadwell, Stepney and Whitechapel there lived a large population of Jews who had fled from persecution in Russia or Poland in the late nineteenth and early twentieth century. Just 'over the bridge' there was a Jewish café, followed by a series of Jewish shops. A little further on there was the Jewish market¹ which flourished until the Second World War.

Jews were unofficially prohibited from setting foot in Wapping. This was a longstanding tradition which had existed many years before the fascist movement led by Oswald Mosley in the thirties. Everybody from Wapping knew the saying which went: 'No Jews allowed down Wapping'. These words were also made into a song which any local could sing:

> When I think about it they used to skip in school to 'No Jews allowed down Wapping' … I probably skipped meself to it.
>
> Doris (born 1923)

Peggy remembered that there had been a large slogan 'No Jews down Wapping' on the wall at Tobacco Dock in Wapping during the thirties, and that children used to smash eggs in the Jewish grocer's just outside Wapping.

Wapping was certainly a no-go area for Jews before the Second World War. Esther, a Jewish woman who grew up ½ mile away, was warned by her parents that going into Wapping was a 'no-no' and that, while you would be unlikely to be physically attacked, you would have to cope with verbal abuse. Ernie, commented:

> One [a Jew] used to have *the nerve* to come down selling bagels.
>
> Ernie (born 1913)

This attitude was in line with the generally held belief that:

> Wapping is for Wapping people only.
>
> Kathleen (born 1934)

Sometimes however, Jews simply had to come into Wapping:

> They had to come over the bridge to go to the hospital and they used to be afraid to come over the bridge.
>
> Ernie (born 1913)

On Sundays, when Jewish people visited their relatives in the hospital, they sometimes even went as far as summoning the police to protect them from the locals.

There was one exception to this general separation between Jew and Gentile: a young woman from a Catholic family in Wapping had fallen in love with a Russian Jewish stallholder at the Jews' Market. At the time (around the first decade of the twentieth century) the couple had had to face tremendous opposition from both their families. Despite this, they went through with the wedding, greatly helped by the girl's many brothers who were at the ready to defend the family honour with their fists if need be. The whole business was enormously stressful for both families, with the tensions gradually subsiding by the time their children went to school:

> There was one family, and everyone accepted him. He lived in the same block as I lived. Yeah, she was a nice lady, she was a Catholic although she married a Jewish feller.
>
> Lizzie (born 1927)

Very likely there were other people with Jewish blood living in Wapping who had integrated with the British through intermarriage and kept quiet about their Jewish origins. Annie had Jewish grandparents but had been brought up without any Jewish influences:

> We weren't Jewish – I mean, the fact that we had a Jewish name but that didn't [qualify] us as being Jews, I mean my mother wasn't a Jew and my father wasn't brought up as a Jew, although they would have been a Jewish family coming over from Europe.
>
> Annie (born 1925)

Reflecting on the anti-Semitism that prevailed in Wapping during her youth, Doris recalled that people blamed the Jews for bringing diseases such as smallpox into the country from Russia. As is generally the case with racism, fear was founded on ignorance, which in turn was perpetuated by the segregation of the communities. Just as people in Wapping aggressively maintained Wapping's boundaries, so the Jewish community was equally keen to exclude 'goys' or gentiles. Their religion and way of life was distinct from that of other East Enders: Whitechapel on a Saturday was filled with Jewish people dressed in their Sabbath best for the synagogue and most Jewish families observed Jewish religious festivals and customs, sending their children to 'shul' (the synagogue) where they learned the religions texts in Hebrew. Despite these barriers, some mixing between Jew and Gentile was inevitable. Many people from Wapping came across Jews in their daily lives, finding themselves working for Jewish bosses in factories and small businesses. By the twenties and thirties, many Jews had risen out of the depths of poverty and were somewhat better off than the majority of the docking families. They had established themselves mainly in the clothing industry, in small businesses and workshops and as market traders and shop-keepers. Ernie's first job was working for Jackson and Joseph, a Jewish boot and shoe manufacturer's off Brick Lane. Mary worked for many years in a small Jewish tailoring firm, Ethel worked with many Jews in a cigar factory and Doris was personal secretary to Jewish solicitor in the City. What was most striking was the warmth with which most people remembered their working relations:

> I used to work for a Jewish man in tailoring, and that was before the Second World War. He gave me a beautiful coat when I got married! ... they were very, very good people, you know.
>
> Mary (born 1912)

Ted also remembered the generosity of the Jewish publican he worked for:

> I used to get all the beer up for him and store it in, and they called me 'Irish Jew'... He used to, when the blokes were, years ago, when they were hard up, he used to give them half a crown, you know, to buy them over their day, to get some food, did old Nat Levy.
>
> Ted (born 1926)

Jews also had nicknames such as 'Sid the Yid'. Doris, who had skipped to the tune of 'No Jews allowed down Wapping' as a child, had nothing but praise for her boss who had looked after her in times of trouble:

> All my life I've been in with these people ... they were Jewish, but it didn't make no difference, I mean he knew I was a Catholic, I mean he's brought me things from Israel – rosaries and anything from a Catholic shop, you know, so when people keep saying about them, I know how kind and good they were to me.
>
> Doris (born 1923)

Many people in Wapping had had some contact with Jews as children when they did jobs for them on the Sabbath:

When they were very frum – that's like, religious, they wouldn't light their fire or put on their lights on Friday. You used to have to do it for them and they'd treat you – give you a couple of bob or something to give to your mother … you could feed the family for that – yeah, but see, they had a few bob and all.

Peggy (born 1920)

We always used to light the fires when we were young, you know, Friday night or Saturday morning you'd light the fires because they weren't allowed to strike a match or anything. But they were very good to us, you know, they'd give you, say, thruppence or some would give you a cake of mozza, yeah. Others give you sixpence, it all depends.

Tom (born 1923)

He gave the family a good service:

Oh, yes, come back at, say, seven o'clock, put another shovel of coal on. Yeah, oh, they was good.

Tom (born 1923)

Whilst there were almost no Jewish workers in the docks and no Jewish shopkeepers in Wapping itself, there was an abundance of grocers and other Jewish food shops very close by. Many people used the Jewish shops just outside Wapping owned by first or second generation immigrants with names such as Sam and Sadie Goldberg, Sam Silbermann or surnames with Russian or Polish endings such as 'vitch' or 'ski'. Audrey mentioned that Jews bartered for goods in their shops:

There was a fruiterer at the top of Wapping Lane – Old Gravel Lane, as it was called then, called 'Sam' and his fruit was very good … It was only just over the bridge – When we were open, they were shut, and when we were shut, they were open so it worked quite well really.

Audrey (born 1927)

People developed good relationships with the shopkeepers:

They all knew our family, the O'Learys! They knew the O'Learys. 'You don't know the *O'Learys?!*' – cos we were a big family.

Tom (born 1923)

The Jews' Market was very popular and Jewish foods had definitely established themselves in Wapping households:

You used to have great big barrels with herrings in, pickled herrings, and they'd get 'em out and slice 'em all up in bagels and give some onion with the herrings … You used to have herrings and all, Sunday for your tea with your cockles and winkles … The Jews used to do lovely wallies there You'd have a wally with your half of fish and chips.[2]

Lizzie (born 1927)

Jack was an enthusiastic expert on Jewish foods remembering, amongst many other things, how he used to choose a live chicken for slaughter in the market. There was a rabbi in the slaughterhouse who blessed the chicken before it was killed:

There used to be Hessel Street, a Jewish market, and we used to go there Sunday morning and we used to get six bagel, a challa, six onion rolls, six horseshoes, go down, pick out a chicken – it would be gutted by the time we got down to the bottom, killed, gutted, pricked and the chicken fat would be there, half a dozen pickled herrings, a cucumber – haimishes, what we call 'greens' (the best is the greens, not the haimisches) and as you go down there, my uncle, who was a thief, he would get a load of stuff and put it in me bag.[3]

Jack (born 1924)

People bartered for their chosen chicken in butcher's shops, where it was plucked and quartered.

People in Wapping rarely seemed to go as far as making friends with Jewish people. Mary was probably rather an exception, since her family already had a lot of Jewish contacts before they moved into Wapping:

There was a café up the top of Wapping Lane, a Jewish family I was very friendly with, and two of their daughters, they were nice singers.

Mary (born 1912)

However, when people worked with Jews they sometimes went to their social functions. Ethel mentioned that her husband had attended a 'Levayer' – a Jewish funeral, to which all the work colleagues of the deceased would have been invited.

As the two cultures mingled, Yiddish words started to creep into the vocabulary of non-Jews. Jack, who moved from Wapping, found himself surrounded by Jews as neighbours:

Wonderful people everybody! And when we moved into Newark Street (I speak very good Yiddish…and we was the only Christians in the turning) and they treated us like *lords* … With Jews there'd always be a chicken at the side of the door, whoosh – garlic whoosh – sausage – I love it![4] … We'd give her £1 a week and there'd be tails and everything else, and eggs, chicken fat.

Jack (born 1924)

One thing that Jewish people shared with cockneys was their sense of humour:

Now there's a race! They were the most natural comedians they were, the Jews. It flowed out of them. I mean, I like the Jews – I liked the Jews.

Tom (born 1923)

At the political level there was, as is well known, a lot of racial tension in the East End during the thirties fomented by Oswald Mosley, leader of the British Union of Fascists, and opposed by socialists, which at the time included the Labour Party and the Communists. Although the hot spots of fascist activity were in Bethnal Green, Shoreditch, Bow and Poplar, there were heated meetings and demonstrations just outside Wapping too:

When I was a boy it was terrible. I used to go down Watney Street, I was twelve, thirteen and they come marching – they were selling the paper, the fascist paper, starting with the Jews, throwing pigs' heads in the synagogues – it was terrible. And right thugs they was. There'd be terrible fights in Dellow Street[5] where they used to speak, but I see Mosley when I was about twelve or thirteen. I used to watch sometimes and see Mosley get up on the platform with Jeffrey Hamm – he was his understudy – and he was preaching against the Jews.

Jack (born 1924)

Several people had witnessed the Battle of Cable Street when they were young adults or children. Jack reflected that the dockers stood by the Jews out of a sense of sympathy, because many of them had also suffered discrimination when they had settled in London:

Most people left Ireland in the potato famine. They got here and they dug the docks out… and I remember when I was a boy, there used to be a notice up 'No Irish need apply' I can remember, oh, yes, in England, 'No Irish apply' … for work, for any job … if it ain't for the dockers, 1936 – we stopped it – not me, I was a boy, but our blokes stopped it, the dock workers stopped it, not the Jews.

Jack (born 1924)

Mosley also used propaganda against the Jews to try to divide public opinion during the Second World War in an attempt to bring people onto Hitler's side, using the slogan 'We won't fight a Jewish war'. This made little impact. On the contrary, according to Frank Lewey, Mayor of Stepney at the time, the War had the opposite effect of uniting people:

In fact Hitler did a surprising thing in his London Blitz, and one that could not have been his intention: he battered down the barriers between Jew and Gentile more in six months than had been done here in the previous fifty years.

Cockney Campaign p. 76.

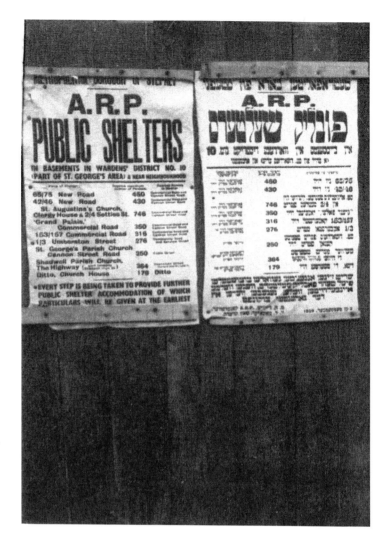

Wapping Boatyard notice, 1939. The notice regarding air-raid precautions is in English and Yiddish. It is an indication that the Second World War helped to break down the barriers between Jews and the people of Wapping. (Kind permission John Joslin)

Notes

1. The Jewish Market was in Hessel Street, just off Cannon Street Road.
2. Pickled cucumbers.
3. A challah was 'A braided loaf of white bread glazed with egg white, very soft and delicate in flavour.' Leo Rosten, *The Joys of Yiddish.*
4. By 'whoosh', he means 'wurst', from the German for 'sausage'.
5. Dellow Street is about 200 yards out of Wapping, joining Cable Street to the Highway.

16

TWO WORLD WARS

The First World War

The destiny of people born in the first two decades of the twentieth century was shaped, or rather hijacked, by the two World Wars. Everybody had his own story to tell, and although only the oldest could remember the First World War, its legacy left a scar on every family.

In Wapping, as in other parts of the country, there was a strong recruitment drive. Ted described the experience of his older brother:

> Well, at the outbreak of War (cos he was in the Guards) they come round the dock and said 'Sign up here' ... they all signed up for so much a week ... well there was such a shimozzel – half of them didn't have uniforms, half of them didn't have rifles and half of them never knew one end from the other end of one.
>
> Ted (born 1926)

Fortunately there was no damage from air raids in Wapping during the First World War, although there were Zeppelin attacks on other parts of the docks.[1] Tower Bridge was raised during air raids, and a policeman rode a bicycle through the streets of Wapping, carrying a notice board which read 'Take cover':

> In St Bride's [dock], they used to have two lights just like road signals, and sometimes Dad used to look out the window there, and he used to say to Mum 'Come on, the amber light's up'. They'd put amber lights up for a warning, then if they was nearer (the German planes) they'd put a red light up.
>
> Mary (born 1912)

Mary was only three years old when she saw a Zeppelin catch fire in the sky. This was her earliest memory and, reliving it in her nineties, she said that it had haunted her all her life. It was an afternoon like any other. She was sitting on the front step with her mother and her aunt who were having a chat with the neighbours:

> All of a sudden my aunt shouted out 'Look quick!' and because she jumped up and pulled me up I can remember it as if it was yesterday. This Zeppelin hit, broke right in half and I see the two men like that – arms and legs – and I can never get that off my mind ... and they were falling face downwards, and I could see it as plain as anything. They fell out of it cos it went in half ... and it was alight. I think they brought the airship down in Cuffley when they hit it.
>
> Mary (born 1912)

Audrey remembered being told about the event by her mother, who had also seen the ball of fire in the sky. There had been two fourteen year old youths in the Zeppelin who were burnt to death.[2]

The many amputees were a painful reminder to everyone of the lives ruined by war. To add insult to injury, men who had returned from the War and could not find work, went round in groups begging.[3] Tragedy hit some families particularly hard:

Above: Interior of George Warner's barber's shop, No. 103 Old Gravel Lane, *c.* 1914. The poster on the wall reads 'Your King and Country Need You – Join The Army Today!' (Copyright Tower Hamlets Local History Library)

Right: Young soldier in First World War uniform. He was killed on 11 November 1918, two hours before the Armistice.

Mrs Green had two sons who enlisted in the early days of the War, and by a strange coincidence they have each lost a leg, Charlie the right and Joseph the left.

(Parish records, St Peter's Church)

There were enough soldiers from Wapping who had been wounded in the services for Father Wainwright to commission a charabanc belonging to a Miss Hornby for a trip to Ham. According to Jack, there were several fatherless boys like him in his school. As fate would have it, Jack was also to become a victim of war. In 1944 he was seriously wounded on D-Day in Normandy. There were many First World War widows and spinsters who had never married because there were not enough men to go round, or because their fiancé had died on 'Flanders fields'. Bill reckoned that this was why his block of flats was always very quiet:

> A lot of them were old women living on their own, so of course they didn't make a noise.

Bill (born 1926)

Children were disturbed by seeing the psychological after-effects of the First World War on some adults:

> You used to have a lady walk round – she'd walk all round Wapping shouting out ... She'd have this high hat on, you know, how the suffragettes dressed. They used to say that she lost her husband in the war.

Lizzie (born 1927)

Coming into contact with shell-shocked adults in the neighbourhood made a deep impression on children:

> It's like the other things we saw at night ... that man who committed suicide in the next block, the Scotch bloke, he gassed himself ... and they brought him out, like – they said it was the shells.

Lizzie (born 1927)

No-body liked to talk much about the suffering they had experienced during the First World War. Ted thought that his father must have come close to starvation when he was captured by the Germans at sea. Norman's father clammed up when the subject of his First World War experiences came up:

> He just said to me once when I couldn't eat, he said 'When you're hungry you'll eat anything!' And that's about all – that's all I got off of him.

Norman (born 1919)

The Second World War

As the conduit for one-third of the nation's trade and supplies, the Port of London was one of the highest priorities for the German air offensive. Indeed the docks were attacked more ferociously than any other civilian target in an attempt to bring the nation to a standstill. Following the onset of the Blitz on 7 September 1940, London was bombed for *seventy-six* successive nights (with the exception of one night of bad weather) during which time one-third of the warehousing of the Port of London Authority went up in flames. The terror endured by the people of Wapping during the sustained enemy attacks is hard to imagine. The Mayor of Stepney, Frank Lewey, wrote a lively and detailed contemporaneous account of the events of the Blitz in his book, *Cockney Campaign*, which helps to give an overview.

Before war was declared, people suspected that German spies were about in the East End, and that ships docking in Wapping were harbouring them:

> That Irish man, Haw Haw – you'd put on the radio – he used to say 'They'll have bombed this place and that place' and they were actually places in Wapping weren't they, like Monza Street and New Crane. They never got bombed but they got mentioned. Well, they had their spies didn't they.[4]

Doris (born 1923)

Annie's younger sister wrote down some of her memories as a child in Wapping in 1939:

I remember that school was preparing for evacuation should the War start. We went to be fitted with gas masks and were told if War came to always carry our gas masks with you, which was all quite exciting to a child. I remember my mother making curtains in black to cover the windows and seeing buses with strips of tape over their windows and lampposts with small bulbs facing downwards. It all seemed very odd at the time but we got used to it—all quite exciting really.

Flo (born c. 1927)

In 1939 the government organised an evacuation scheme for children whose parents wished it. St Patrick's School issued this memorandum to parents:

Please notice that anybody who fills in the Government forms about possible evacuation should write the word 'Catholic' in large block letters at the top, so that the Authority may know how many Catholic children have to be provided for.

Children were taken to Guildford and Brighton with their schools. When it came to it, some parents, like Ted's, could not face parting with their children and withdrew them from the scheme at the last minute.

In Annie's family three of the children were evacuated all the way to Cornwall as soon as war was declared. While two of the siblings had good experiences, the other sister came home early:

I hated it, although the lady we lived with was very kind. The local people treated us like we came from a different planet. I feel my parents were right to send us away but I had changed from a child to a young adult and my relationship with my parents was a bit strained for a while.

Violet (born c. 1928)

Bill had been quite put out when his mother came to bring him back to Wapping:

It was quite good at Brighton. I was allocated to a Mrs M. and she was an old lady, an old widow but she did everything for me, you know. I was a little kid about 'so' high and she did everything for me! She even cleaned my shoes for me which was unusual – I usually had to do that meself!

Bill (born 1926)

Later he was sent away again:

I was staying with some people who worked on a small farm and they had these large shire horses, you know, the great big things – I thought they were marvellous! That was the best thing about the whole place.

As time went on, however, he grew more and more ill at ease with the family as he and their son were sleeping in the same room as the parents:

Well maybe one or both of them couldn't carry on their married life, so things gradually got a bit worse – little bit of trouble in school, you know, with bullying, so one day I thought 'Well, if Saturday turns out to be a bright, warm day, I'm going to go for a walk.' so I walked into Newbury, got on a train and came back home.

Bill (born 1926)

The Blitz began on 7 September 1940 on a sunny Saturday afternoon. A dock master living at Wapping Pierhead gazed into the sky and tried to count the number of German planes flying over the docks. He gave up after 140 as there were plenty more behind. There were countless fires as seven-storey warehouses, cranes and barges burst into flames. Firewatchers reported unexploded incendiaries hanging from the rigging of ships. Annie, aged fourteen, was on her way out of Wapping to collect her father's trousers from the cleaner's the afternoon the Blitz started:

All of a sudden, as I reached the bridge, the siren sounded. Now I wasn't frightened because we'd been used to them coming over and nothing happening, and I stood there for about ten minutes, and I thought, because the bridge would go up – they all went up – and I thought 'Shall I go back home or shall I chance it and go across?' I decided to go back home and it was just as well I did.

Annie (born 1925)

The bridges were all raised whenever an air raid threatened, as a precaution against damage to dock access points; the result of this was that it was not possible to leave Wapping in the usual way during attacks. Annie would not have been able to return to Wapping if she had crossed the bridge:

My father hurried my mother and I to the wharf where we were to shelter … The whole of the wharves was alight. It was a ring of fire … being an air-raid warden, he then left us to assist the elderly, infirm, young and mothers with babies into the shelters. And I can remember my Mum having hysterics, cos she was very young – she was only thirty-two. For two solid hours without remit we were bombarded with high-explosive bombs. We could hear them dropping and the building shook to each impact. There is no adequate way to describe the feeling – it was truly horrific. We were ringed with fire and my father knew he had to get us out as soon as possible which was not easy as the bridges were still up. Eventually we managed to get a large black cab shared with about ten other people to Tower Bridge from where we walked across by a narrow lock.

Annie (born 1925)

They decided to go and stay with relatives in North London:

But before we could leave, the sirens sounded again. This time we sheltered in the basement of a dress shop, along with somewhere around a hundred others. We were packed in like sardines and had to stand up all night long … when we came out in the morning the place was absolutely dreadful – the smoke and firemen and the smell.

Annie (born 1925)

Three days later she returned to Wapping with her mother:

This was on the Saturday, so on the Tuesday morning – we hadn't got any clothes or anything like that – no toothbrushes … The stench of burning, the dirt and the sight of the destroyed buildings was quite frightening, but there was worse. As we got to the bridge there were some neighbours getting evacuated and one of them shouted out to my mother 'Where're you going, Mrs Jacobs?' She said 'Oh we're just going to collect some clothes because …' and this lady said 'Don't bother!'. When we got to the Milk Yard, there was the flat demolished, so there was nothing to get.

Annie (born 1925)

Theirs happened to be the only flat destroyed in the building.[5] According to George who saw it being bombed, there was not a single person there at the time – just one Pekinese dog!

There was never any other one touched, just ours and there was a complete hole there … I held my Mum's hand, as she was crying, you see, and I said 'Don't cry, Mummy' I said 'because at least we weren't there' and she looked down at me and she said 'No, you don't understand, dear, but you will when you're a bit older'. And of course, I did, I mean, she'd lost everything she had.

Annie (born 1925)

Lizzie told her story:

We were sheltering down there one night, and they dropped loads of incendiary bombs on Wapping, and they dropped 'em on the roof of where we were and we had to get out, and we all had pillows what we laid on, cos we didn't have tin hats or nothing, and we had to run from there, and we come out from there, and we went under the arch at Jackman House, cos they took all the railings away in the War and we all ran down Greenbank and we got to Dundee Street, and we went in St John's Wharf, and that was the bad night, … and the people who went in Morocco Wharf area, a torpedo hit it and they had to come out of there and come down St John's [Wharf] and that was the night yous[6] jumped out, you got out through the loopholes … we come out next morning and they said all the women and children had to come out of Wapping and we went in an open lorry with some other families and we went down hopping.

Lizzie (born 1927)

George left Wapping on foot with his wife, whose jaws had locked together with fear. Looking back at the river as they headed for South London he saw 'an avenue of flame'.

After that it was too dangerous for people to stay in Wapping. By the following Monday, the town clerk of Stepney had arranged for 1,000 homeless shelterers to be evacuated by river steamer from Wapping to Richmond. Doris remembered the panic and confusion. She was told:

'You gotta get on the boats' – they were clearing Wapping. We got on these barges. Well, a friend of mine, her father was a warden. I said, 'Where're we going, Mau?', 'Oh we're going to Windsor'. We didn't, we landed at Kew and they didn't want us – all Londoners! They did *not* want us!

Doris (born 1923)

Lizzie had had a terrifying experience when leaving Wapping:

They said all the women and children had to come out of Wapping, and we went in an open lorry with some other families and we went down hopping. I got machine gunned down. We got in a ditch. We could see him, he come so low, we could see him and when we got off the lorry, when we were going down there that day, we got off and they used to call it 'dog fighting' in the sky – stopping the planes to get to London – and this plane, we reckoned, it had no more bombs, and it come down, and it machine-gunned all up the road. We all laid in the ditches. My sister got stung with stinging nettles.

Lizzie (born 1927)

Some people left Wapping and stayed away for the duration:

I was in March, Cambridgeshire. I was there for about five years with the children. My family used to come down and see me and they gave me a two-bedroom cottage and I was alright down there and the people were ever so good to me.

Nellie (born 1916)

For Lilly and her family, evacuation meant going from the frying pan into the fire:

They took us on the trains to Leicester. I think it took us all day long to get there – over the bombing. When we did get there, they were marvellous ... they gave us food, they gave us everything ... Anyway then they found a big house ... as I say, the authorities were so good, they supplied us with bedding, utensils and I think we had about sixteen camp beds – it looked like an army hospital. I think it was the first night we was in there, my mother said (this was Leicester) 'Come to the Post Office with me' ... we went to the Post Office; well, I tell you, it was rather late because it was dark, I think it must have been about six-ish, and as we come back, we walked in the passage and through the fan light, we could see lights all lighting up: Germans! – they bombed Leicester – well, that was the night they bombed Coventry and where they had to let their bombs go was all on Leicester. Terrible night! Well, we had to all come out of the house, and we went into a school opposite. We was in there *all night long* so you can imagine – they erected emergency toilets – it was a nightmare. Safety?! And next morning we all came home!

Lilly (born 1925)

Others went to and from the hop fields in the autumn of 1940 but this was dangerous as there were air-raids even there and travelling was hazardous:

We stayed there [in Kent] for a month but the men used to come down of a night at the weekend, and some of the girls who didn't come away with their Mum, they'd come down and all, but they used to go home Sunday night and this little lot went home ... they got on this bus to bring 'em round to Tower Bridge, then walk down the steps to go to Wapping, and the bus got hit by a landmine and there was just one man come out of that bus alive, all the others got killed and he lost his eye.

Lizzie (born 1927)

Wapping was almost fully repopulated well before the end of the War. People who had lost their homes went to stay with relatives, friends, or neighbours until they were re-housed somehow by the council. Audrey remembered returning to her house:

> After the first part of the Blitz when we had no water, gas or electricity, we had to go and stay with my uncle in Hampshire and when we came back after a month or two, things had settled down and the door had been blown off, so anybody could walk in, but there was nothing taken. It was all there including some money my mother had left in a drawer and forgotten to take. So there was no looting – when people talk about looting during the Blitz, but there was certainly no looting here in Wapping.
>
> Audrey (born 1927)

Those people who chose to stay in Wapping endured the most appalling danger night after night:

> And many a night we had to run, because of the incendiary bombs, and we'd have to run either all the way over here to St John's – you've got no idea—see this little door? [pointing out of her window] that went down to the basement, and I think it was three floors deep – very, very deep. If a bomb fell on it we would have been buried alive … Well I can remember one night, we had to come out of the Watson's shelter, they said 'Go round to Colonial Wharf' and I was running along because everyone was – it was survival, and I turned the corner and I can remember, I got thrown flat to the ground: a bomb had fallen on British and Foreign Wharf, and there was a couple of locals got killed then. And then another night … I'd be running across the bridge … the nuns was out there putting sand on incendiary bombs: they were still burning. *Burning!*
>
> Lilly (born 1927)

Soldiers on leave were overheard saying that it was safer at the Front than at home in Wapping.

Air Raid Precaution wardens and other civilians, including many women, risked their lives putting out fires and rescuing others from burning buildings, digging them out of rubble and rescuing them from flying debris. There were several civilian volunteers who died in Wapping whilst working for the heavy rescue team:

> Their main thing was, anybody trapped in the building, they would dig 'em out, jack the wall up and he was a driver on one of them, and a bomb came over, dropped right in … and he was killed outright. Poor old Mr Clark.
>
> Ted (born 1926)

A civilian rescue team formed in Wapping became particularly famous for their heroism. Led by Patsie Duggan, they called themselves 'The Dead End Kids'.[7] Basing themselves at Watson's Wharf which they used as a fire-watching station, they saved countless lives by sending out members of their teams to extinguish fires. Although only in their teens (the youngest member was Patsie's sister, aged only thirteen) they were extremely efficient, well equipped and extraordinarily courageous.

From the outbreak of the War, local firms had been applying to the council for financial assistance to convert warehouse basements into air-raid shelters. Anderson shelters provided by the Government were of no use to people with large families living in flats or tenement blocks. On the first night of bombing, many people fled to the basements of the wharves which were damp and musty and sometimes full of inflammable material such as hemp. George remembered diving for cover as soon as he realised the Germans were flying over. Pure fear had obliterated the noise of the planes as he ran for shelter into Oliver's Wharf. He stayed there all night, sleeping on bags of peppercorns with rats' tails brushing his face. The following morning, he emerged with a very red nose after sneezing all night long because of the pepper.

Mary's mother had been blown through her living room door by a bomb blast before there were any shelters. Miraculously she was uninjured. When firemen came to the rescue, she flatly refused to leave her home.

Little by little, the wharves were adapted as shelters. In other parts of London people fled to the Underground, but in Wapping the Underground had to be closed because it went under the river and there would have been a danger of flooding. Doris used to go to the large shelter at St John's Wharf in the early stages of the War:

The 'Dead End Kids'. Their leader was Patsie Duggan and their headquarters was at Watson's shelter. The other members were Jackie Duggan, Fred Pope, Ronnie Doyle, Harold Parker, Eddie Chusonis, Joe Storey, Terry Connolly, Graham Bath, Ronnie Eyres, Oswald Bath, Bert Eden and Maureen Duggan (who joined aged thirteen). They saved many lives fire-fighting in the Blitz. Ronnie Eyres and Bert Eden were killed by bombs. Patsie was wounded but still carried on. (Every attempt to obtain permission for reproducing this photograph has been made)

Well, we sat out on wooden seats all night, because they weren't prepared here for war, really. And then after that they did bunks, didn't they.

Doris (born 1923)

As the War went on, sheltering became a way of life.

My Dad was a bit of a conman. He worked on the market. Many times in the War he got chased down Nightingale Lane on his bike, he's got chicken or meat or fish hanging round his neck … I remember when we was all in there—used to be the Hermo[8] that was the shelter we was in, and loads and loads of us used to be there, and we all took turns up there, but me Dad, working in the market used to pinch the giblets and me Mum used to make big tins of stew and bowls of stew and take it there and everybody took their turn.

Kathleen (born 1934)

The Hermitage was one of the bigger shelters and the people who used it formed a committee with the aim of making life as 'comfortable and happy and healthy as possible.'[9] A resolution was passed to stop children from gambling and to prevent gate-crashers from entering. The night before the shelter was evacuated because of bombing, they managed to organise a party for the children. People sang songs and tried to distract themselves in the shelters:

We was down at the Metropolitan Wharf next to the Prospect of Whitby.[10] Perhaps a fellow would be playing a flute or a mouth organ or something like that.

Ron (born 1921)

Habitués of larger shelters laid claim to their regular pitches. Members of the clergy visited the shelters every night and took services there. Dr Hannah Billig also visited the shelters regularly to attend to the sick. Mary's family was lucky enough to occupy a large shelter in a wharf:

She [Mary's mother] had a wardrobe down there, she had her bed – well, the springs off her bed and the overlay, an electric fire, electric kettle – we never went short of anything while we was down there! And you know, she used to make it as much like home as she could.

Mary (born 1912)

They shared it with the family of a publican who was buried in his cellar when his pub was hit.[11]

Many other people in Wapping sheltered in the basements of their flats which they had adapted for the purpose:

One time, number one Willoughby House was made into a shelter – you know, they put long pieces of wood between the floor and the ceiling [which] held it up; the windows were taken out and big boxes were put outside the windows filled with soil, so the only ventilation in there was the front door, if it was open.

Bill (born 1926)

People slept in these stifling conditions on bunk beds. Lizzie recalled the routine:

They emptied all the bottom of those Franklin and Frobisher[12] … and then we all had a spot where we went and we used to take our bedclothes, roll our bedclothes up and our gasmasks, and we used to go down there of a night, and we all laid down there … Course we didn't know who was clean, and we used to end up with fleas in our house and all that.

Lizzie (born 1927)

Others preferred to risk their lives sleeping in their own bed. When they got up the morning after a raid, they did not know what they would find:

Because there were so many people you knew that got killed, you know. You got the news the next morning 'Oh so and so was killed' … there were lots of people who were there who suddenly vanished.

Doris (born 1923)

Everybody could bring to mind a friend, neighbour or relative who had been killed during this period. People would say 'Don't tell me another bomb story!' Survival was a matter of chance. Ethel's husband had a lucky escape. After he had been for a drink with a friend, he ran one way out of the pub, the friend the other way. His friend was killed. After a night in a shelter, people tried to carry on with their lives as normally as possible:

You'd just wash your face and go to work. Oh, you might have had a couple of hours sleep but how can you sleep in your clothes? You was just in your clothes. But we just used to have to get on with it because if you didn't go to work, you got no money – you had to go to work, bombs are falling or not … You'd still get up and walk through the rubble, and then you had to bring your little bit of wages home, because no-one would *give* you any money.

Peggy (born 1920)

We used to go to work with all the bombs flying and that … I can always remember around the Bank all the hose pipes when there was a big fire[13] … I remember coming down the Lane, Old Gravel Lane, in those days it was called, and there was a guard, an Air Raid Warden – we were petrified trying to come down the Lane, couldn't get there quick enough, you know, and everybody said, 'S'all right, Els, you're alright, your Mum's alright, not a cut's done.

Elsie (born 1913)

The cinemas were always packed, with people doggedly turning a deaf ear to the warnings from the air-raid sirens. Going to the pub was also a welcome distraction from reality. The Town of Ramsgate owned a huge grey cat which they claimed was the largest cat in London. Somehow or other (with the help of a parrot) it raised thousands of pounds for charity. Most shops had to close in the face of the dangers. At least one family however, managed to run a grocer's shop and keep a pub open throughout the bombing, and there was a baker who cooked Sunday dinners for those who stayed in Wapping throughout the war. Elsie's family was obliged to leave:

We got bombed right out, just by our shop. It was on the corner, it was right by the dock wall, the dock there round the top of Penang Street. Course there was all the fire, and they come down and took us right away, so during the War we were more or less down at Barnehurst.

Elsie (born 1913)

Father Luetchford, Vicar of St Peter's Church, wrote a detailed account of what it was like in Wapping during this period of heavy bombardment:

15.10.1940: for many days no water could be had except from buckets which were carried round the streets and gas could not again be laid on. Railway Station didn't function for a time. The Mission House was bombed. Three sisters went to St George's hospital … But Sister Catherine was killed instantly by a torpedo. The Clergy House was badly damaged.

When St Peter's Church was bombed:

Mass was celebrated next morning at 7.30 and 8 in the midst of indescribable filth.

A 'feeding centre' was opened for people who had been bombed out or had no gas or water:

25.12.1940. Feeding Centre in the Senior School – 60 people attended Xmas dinner. The Minister of Food visited the Feeding Centre in the morning.

Father Luetchford's diary, St Peter's Church archive

The Blitz raged on for eight months; the last bombing in that phase of the War was on 10 May 1941.
    After the Blitz there was no more bombing for three years during which people tried to pick up the threads of normal life in an uneasy lull. Women spent hours queuing for rations:

In Wapping Lane there used to be a shop, there, I forget the name now of it, but my sister next to me, she never worked, she had two children and she'd line up for my Mum and used to get two sausages on her book …

Lizzie (born 1927)

Naturally there was the black market:

It was a bit hard, but then my Mum got in with the Jews … a nice Jew lady in Watney Street, Annie, and if anything was going, see, and if you had the money to pay and all, she used to say Mrs Walker, I've got so-and-so and so-and-so.

Lizzie (born 1927)

People living by the docks may have managed a bit better with rationing than most:

Well, of course, I managed like everybody else. We got by – sometimes we'd have good weeks – if the boats got in …

Ethel (born 1916)

Well, there was a lot of things went on – there was a lot of 'fiddle me dear' as you call it – you never went without tea because of the tea warehouses and Middleton's used to do all the sugar but even if it was the demerara sugar, not the white sugar but you could put that in your tea.

Ted (born 1926)

Family life was often completely disrupted: many mothers were called up for war work whilst their sons and husbands were serving in the forces. Ted could not wait to join up:

A friend I went to school with, Patrick Molloy, we both put our ages up and joined the Armed Guards. You were supposed to be getting on for eighteen but they didn't worry – but we was sixteen.

Ted (born 1926)

St John's Church after it was bombed, 1941. (Copyright Tower Hamlets Local History Library)

Later Ted was sent into active service where he survived some truly terrible experiences:

> I was in the Royal Engineers and we was down in Italy putting bridges up and as soon as you made a noise, the Germans used to start shooting you, and I'm afraid many a time you'd need a new pair of pants with the shells coming over ... and we used to lift mines, lay mines and blow things up.
>
> Ted (born 1926)

Joining the army gave many people new opportunities and better health. Jack enjoyed regular meals for the first time in his life:

> When I joined up they had blokes like a bamboo pole. You know what I mean, they were all thin. You got in there and they never knew what a pair of pants was.
>
> Jack (born 1924)

He also reflected that joining the army had diverted him from a life of crime:

> I was always quick-tempered and when I went into the Service I had nothing to do: I wasn't in a week, I ended up in the nick, but I'd like to say to you now ... the greatest thing in the world is the Service and if they done it today, you know, a lot of the young people – there'd be no crime.
>
> Jack (born 1924)

Jack paid a high price for this. His war wounds left him with a disability but at least he survived. Lizzie could list several young men she had known who never returned from war, including one of her brothers:

There was loads of lovely boys round Wapping that went to war and never came back … I had a brother on that Russian convoy … there was Sidney Oakes, he was in coastal command and he got shot down, he used to stop the planes getting to London, Terry Mulligan, he was a gunman on a plane, he got killed. The boy Edwards, me brother, George, one of the twins, he got killed at Dunkirk – he was the first one to be killed.

Lizzie (born 1927)

When fathers eventually returned from the War, it was often difficult for the rest of the family to adjust:

She was born during the War and my husband was a prisoner of war wasn't he, for about four years. When he went away she was a year old; when he came home, she was five and a half and I always remember she used to say 'Who's that man? I don't like that man in here, Mum … You sleep with that man – you used to let *me* sleep with you!

Dolly (born 1912)

During the final year of the War the Germans bombed the East End again with doodlebugs or buzz bombs. People had just eleven seconds from when the engine cut out to when the bomb exploded, in which to run for cover:

I was standing up in Willoughby House when I saw the flying bomb come over and drop on it [the Hermitage]. I saw a few people dug out of the wreckage.

Bill (born 1926)

This bomb fell in Wapping in 1944 killing five members of the ARP rescue service. A further disaster occurred just a few months before the war ended: a V2 rocket hit the Hermitage, this time killing six more people and wounding many others.

Because of this double tragedy in an area of the East End that was so badly damaged, people in Wapping chose this spot to create a war memorial. After a hard–won campaign, there is now a monument and garden on the river front where the Hermitage once stood, commemorating the suffering and fortitude of civilians of East London.[14]

Wapping after the War

At the end of the War, politicians were full of optimism and grand schemes for urban planning, but the immediate priority was rehousing of the homeless.[15] Doris had been caught up in chaos and confusion when she lost her home at the age of seventeen. She had walked back from the shelter to her home only to find the street had been hit by a landmine:

My Mum was saying to me as we were walking along 'Oh, I'll light the fire and put the kettle on and you'll be able to get to work.' And when we got to the corner, you know there was the shop there called 'Kendal's' and the shutters had come down, and I said 'Ooh, what's that!' And then looked across out and it was just flaring…our place upstairs and the people underneath … there were no floors … nothing – all burnt, there was all my father's army things, photographs, *gone*, you know.

She was not eligible for any money from the Unemployment Assistance Board because she was working and was left with just the clothes she stood up in. After a short stay in Kew she came back to Wapping.

… and all you got was £6. I think eventually I had to go somewhere in Poplar … I suppose for clothes … eventually, I was staying with these friends at number 18 …

Doris (born 1923)

Although the docks had started working again in 1944 after trade returned from other ports, many warehouses and factories in and around Wapping were damaged.[16] St Peter's Church and the hospital were badly damaged and all that was left of St John's Church was the tower.

Clement Atlee had been Mayor of Stepney in 1919 and was on a mission to improve the appalling housing conditions and overcrowding that were still afflicting East Enders. In 1938, 90 per cent of people in Stepney had no bathroom and in the new blocks which the London County Council had proudly erected in Wapping in 1932, up to five people were still sharing a bedroom. The challenge of rebuilding was massive. At least children could enjoy playing in the bomb craters and rubble. The LCC bought neglected properties from private landlords and set about demolishing rows of Victorian houses, replacing them with blocks of flats. One man commented that the one good thing Hitler did with his bombing was to get rid of the bugs.

Many young people were forced to move out, often to new towns such as Harlow and Basildon because of the housing shortage. Lizzie had missed her family desperately when she first moved out to Dagenham in 1951, returning to visit her mother twice a week:

> If me husband had said 'Come, we'll go back' I'd have gone back. I used to cry every night when I first went, cos … your Mum and you all lived near one another – like all your brothers and sisters, we all lived near one and other.
>
> Lizzie (born 1927)

There was, of course, no going back, and life slowly began to change. Lorries gradually replaced horses and carts and in the fifties the odd motor car started to appear. Gone was the muffin man and many other street salesmen. More fundamental changes came about: the community network began to loosen as more and more people left and new people from other parts of the country arrived. Some of the locals referred to these newcomers as 'problem families.' In the class Barbara taught in St Peter's School in 1949, there were several children whose fathers were in prison. Marjorie, a social worker in Wapping in 1956, mentioned vandalism as a problem:

> It was very difficult having a car there because little boys from the neighbourhood had a habit of jumping on the roof and having a lark. So my poor old thing became even more battered.

Marjorie had come to work in Wapping in 1956 when, rather unexpectedly, it played a part in world events: of the 200,000 or more refugees fleeing to the West after the Hungarian Uprising, 500 were welcomed into the recently closed hospital of St George's in the East in Wapping where they stayed for six months. Wapping accommodated a complete cross-section of Hungarian society, from members of the aristocracy to gipsies who formed an orchestra of traditional instruments within the hospital for regular Hungarian dances.

> We set up a Hungarian Committee which they elected themselves, and we made them responsible for security, because the 'ladies of the night' in Wapping just flooded in, you see!
>
> Marjorie (social worker in Wapping 1956)

Prior to the War there had almost certainly not been any such ladies in Wapping.

After the refugees left, St George's in the East hospital, once a focal point in the community, stood empty for several years, and was finally demolished in 1963 to make way for a tower block typical of those which were springing up all over the East End.[17] The London Docks were closed a few years later in 1968, essentially as a result of the containerisation of maritime trade. In the late 1970s, some ten years after they had closed, the docks were filled in, marking the final farewell to what had been the raison d'être of Wapping. As Victor commented:

> It's a good life down there, it's like a village community in Wapping, it seems like a village on its own once you get over the bridges – or it used to be. The bridges don't swing no more.
>
> Victor (born 1930)

Notes

1. In 1915 seven people were killed in a Zeppelin attack.
2. The Zeppelin was shot down by William Leefe-Robinson on 2 September 1916. There was a massive fire caused by the hydrogen, which was visible from a distance of over 100 miles. William Leefe-Robinson died in the great influenza epidemic in 1918.
3. Grace Foakes, *My Part of the River*.
4. William Joyce, known as Lord Haw Haw, was born in Ireland, came over to Britain and joined the Fascist Party and was active in the local elections in Stepney with Moseley in 1938. He fled to Germany in 1939 where he worked for Göbbels' propaganda department and was hanged for treason by the British in 1946.
5. Riverside Mansions.
6. She is referring to Nellie, who was interviewed with her, and whoever was with Nellie at the time.
7. The Dead End Kids were Patsie Duggan, Fred Pope, Jackie Duggan, Ronnie Doyle, Harold Parker, Eddie Chusonis, Joe Storey, Terry Conolly, Graham Bath, Ronnie Eyres, Oswald Bath, Bert Eden and Maureen Duggan (aged thirteen).
8. Hermitage Wharf, a very large shelter which was subsequently bombed in 1940.
9. *The Hermitage Shelter Minutes*, December 1940.
10. A famous pub in Wapping.
11. The Three Swedish Crowns.
12. 'Franklin' and 'Frobisher' are names of blocks of flats.
13. The Bank of England.
14. Tower Hamlets Local History Library has a list of places in Wapping which were damaged by the War, and also a list of Wapping inhabitants who were killed.
15. The ambitious Abercrombie Plan would give rise to fifteen new satellite towns around London and encourage people to leave the inner city for the suburbs. Industries would not be replaced in Stepney and Wapping but moved out of London. The East End was destined to have green spaces near the riverside for recreation and leisure.
16. Including Meredith & Drew biscuit factory which was never rebuilt, Yeatman's jam factory, Gibbs' soap factory, the British and Foreign Wharf and Orient Wharf.
17. Oswell House.

CONCLUSION

What does this book reveal about the attitudes of people who grew up in Wapping between the two World Wars? How are they different from the generations that followed?

Before the Second World War, people's destiny was far more predetermined by social class than it is today. Interviewees often said that they had had little ambition to change their status, probably because the opportunities to do so were almost non-existent. Tom's self-deprecation was fairly typical:

> I wasn't much of a scholar, really, but I got by though. You get by without money, you know, or without brains! Oh, I got by reading and writing, but any lecturing would go in one ear and out the other. I wish I'd been more acute—[laughs] but there you are: I've been happy in me life.
>
> Tom (born 1923)

The lives of most women were shaped by childbearing and their marital status. Ada was thankful that she was only able to have the one child:

> I never had no more children, did I … But I think that was the making of me, really in a manner of speaking, I 'spose. I've always worked, I've always had to work for my living. I've worked from the age of fourteen 'til I was sixty three.
>
> Ada (born 1909)

Neither men nor women felt they had had much choice or control over the direction of their lives: so many people of their generation were simply concerned with the day-to-day struggle against poverty and hardship. Several people reflected on the effect that growing up in poverty had had on them:

> I never had a new pair of shoes. My mother used to go into a boot menders and anyone – which a lot of people did then – anyone that left shoes and didn't pick 'em up, he'd sell them for about sixpence. It never bothered me, so I've learnt to appreciate all what I've got in the meantime.
>
> Lilly (born 1925)

At the time she had never considered the hardship she was experiencing:

> We didn't know no better, we didn't know no different.
>
> Lilly (born 1925)

Jack had been determined to do better for himself and his family:

> I have come up hard, you know, in the hard way and I always said this: that no way would my wife ever go through with what my mother went through … and I've worked, I've worked every day of my life, you know what I mean – I still get offers of employment – still!
>
> Jack (born 1924)

Several people commented that material possessions do not create happiness. Many people would have agreed with Norman:

> No, meself, I thought we were better off making our own entertainment, because the children today, they've got all this television and these computers and I don't think it's a good thing.
>
> Norman (born 1919)

Some were ambivalent about the benefits of the Welfare State. Tom implied that there was no real need for the NHS:

> Yeah, we roughed it, we came out alright, we all lived to a good age.
>
> Tom (born 1923)

Several people felt that the postwar generation was rather parasitical and over-dependent on the state:

> See, people don't realise how better off they are now and I say that from the bottom of my heart. No matter what the government want to give you, you can't expect money besides to go on holidays … It was a different way of living.
>
> Peggy (born 1920)

On recollecting how her mother had struggled, Lilly echoed this view:

> Not like today. Handed to 'em on a plate … Look what they get today! No wonder they're all having children.
>
> Lilly (born 1925)

Nellie marvelled at the material differences between herself and her grandchildren:

> My Alan, you know, has got a son, Darren, and they've got three boys: Bill's about six – four and three – something like that and they've got a bedroom *each!*
>
> Nellie (born 1916)

Life for this generation of people revolved around the family. People felt that close family networks were sadly lacking in modern society:

> That's what the kids miss I think, today, no family life.
>
> Elsie (born 1913)

> Of a Sunday, we had to go [to visit relatives] and then those cousins of mine, they had to go, they went early and then we'd go down. That's stopped now, ain't it, when you visited your grandparents. It was a regular thing, walking around visiting aunts and uncles and what have you. Gone – something's gone wrong to me – the community like. Oh, I don't know what's going to end up, do you?
>
> Doris (born 1923)

People lamented the decline in community spirit:

> They all helped one another, not like today. They get a few bob and they don't want to know, neighbours.
>
> Dolly (born 1912)

Despite the fact that these people grew up in a far less child-centred world, where there was a strict hierarchy between parent and child and children were brought up to fear authority, people looked back on their childhood with a great deal of nostalgia:

> Really we didn't have half the things children had today, but we did have a happy childhood, even school you know … I've got loads of happy memories.
>
> Lizzie (born 1927)

Some of this was related to a sense of sadness for a way of life that had passed, for example the disappearance of customs such as the funeral wake held in people's homes. Rather strangely perhaps, people were nostalgic about aspects of life that were obviously unpleasant or difficult. Fights in those days belonged to a safer world:

> They'd have a fist fight and then go in the pub and have a drink afterwards, but now these days, they'd want to stab you or shoot you or kick you to death!
>
> Ted (born 1926)

Some people made light of their brushes with serious illness:

> I suppose running a temperature, that's what caused the convulsion fit, but you know we had a lovely life really.
>
> Lizzie (born 1927)

Somehow, despite everything, the world of the past was a happier, more secure and generally better place:

> Because I find it in our society too gloomy. You walk along, you'll see the butcher boy riding a bike, a kid of fifteen, he'll be whistling. There'd be a group of boys, fellers, perhaps eighteen in age, on the corner of a street singing, you know, not offensive, just singing modern songs there were then. But everyone, they was human, they worked hard.
>
> Ron (born 1921)

Lizzie could have been speaking for many of her contemporaries when she said:

> Yes, it was, it was a really colourful, wonderful place, Wapping.
>
> Lizzie (born 1927)

With all their stories, both humorous and painful, the voices of all the people who contributed to this book have brought that world to life again.

AFTERWORD

The people in this book

ADA was born in 1909 and lived in Wapping all her life. A few years ago there was a terrible fire next to her block of flats and she had to be evacuated. She took this in her stride, saying it was just like the Blitz all over again.

DOLLY was born in 1912. She lived in Wapping all her life until her late eighties when she had to move to a home because she was too frail to look after herself. Her first words to me were 'I'm finished now'.

MARY was born in 1912, moved to Wapping when she was three and remained in the same flat ever since. A lively and talkative woman, she enjoyed good health in her old age, and the company of her son and daughter-in-law and their dog.

ELSIE was born in 1913. Twice widowed, Elsie remained very active and cheerful until her breathing got so bad that she could not go out any more. Her best friend lived just a few yards away but she also became housebound and so deaf that they could no longer even speak to each other on the telephone.

ERNIE was born in 1913 and lived alone in a council flat. When he heard about the destruction of the Twin Towers on 11 September 2001, he said he was glad that he did not expect to live for much longer.

NELLIE Lizzie's aunt by marriage, was born in 1916. She was one of a large extended family. There were ten other family members for tea on the day of the interview.

ETHEL was born in 1916. She had been active in the Labour Party. Living alone since she was widowed, she felt vulnerable and was anxious about the cuts in the Home Help Service.

NORMAN was born in 1919. Happily married for over fifty years, he and Sal were moved out of Wapping against their will, and missed the community there.

SAL was born in 1925.

PEGGY was born in 1920. She could not bring herself to leave the East End, despite mourning the loss of the community. The nearest she came to going abroad was flying on Concorde, a seventieth birthday treat from her son.

GRACE was born in 1921. She had six children and moved away from the East End when she got married. I interviewed her in a warden-controlled council flat in a small village in Essex. Despite being very hard up, she welcomed me with a slap-up tea.

JANET was born in 1921 into a large Wapping family. She was active in the church and pensioners' club and helped her even more elderly neighbours with their shopping.

RON was born in 1921. A mine of information about the East End, he was also active in a pensioners' club. His flat was full of photographs of his family, including his successful nephews and nieces.

TOM was born in 1923. At the age of seventy-nine he was still working part-time. He said 'It's better than staring at these four walls, isn't it!' In his living room was a photograph of a handsome sailor – his brother who was killed in the Second World War.

DORIS was born in 1923. She lived in Wapping all her life. She was politically active and a local councillor in the fifties. She never married.

JACK was born in 1924. He was proud of his council flat in Stepney where he lived with his wife. He enjoyed using his influence locally, and was always being called upon to do odd jobs, since he could turn his hand to anything practical. Although no longer 24 stone, he was still a large man with a large personality.

LILLY was born in 1925. Nothing would induce Lilly to leave Wapping where she was born. She was very proud of the view from her window, and could point to many landmarks in her story.

ANNIE was born in 1925. She was a widow with four children. They were all in close contact with her – in fact two of them phoned during the interview. Annie completed a university degree in her seventies and regarded learning to use a laptop computer as one of her greatest achievements.

BILL was born in 1926. He lived in Wapping all his life, latterly in a tower block. A keen cyclist in his youth, he kept a bicycle in his hallway which he bought second hand in 1939. He enjoyed real ale, and his interests included wildlife and trains.

TED was born in 1926. He was a pillar of the community, well known and well loved.

LIZZIE was born in 1927. Although she left Wapping in 1951, she visited regularly.

AUDREY was born in 1927. Her family had been in Wapping for many generations and have participated in local politics and church life.

BOB was born in 1933.

KATHLEEN (Bob's wife) was born in 1934. Kathleen's family have been in Wapping for generations, but she and Bob decided to leave to be with their daughter in Kent. They were concerned about the level of teenage crime in Wapping.

BARBARA worked in Wapping as a teacher in 1949.

PAM worked in Wapping as a 'Lady Almoner' in 1956.

With contributions from George, born in 1913, Eric born in 1915, Frank, born in 1919, Esther, born in 1928, Annie's sisters, Flo and Violet, Victor, born in 1930, Eadie, born in 1938, Ethel's daughter, Angie and Marjorie, social worker in Wapping in 1956.

APPENDIX

See map of Wapping and its surroundings overleaf. (Enlargement from Bartholomew's plan of London central area, 1925)

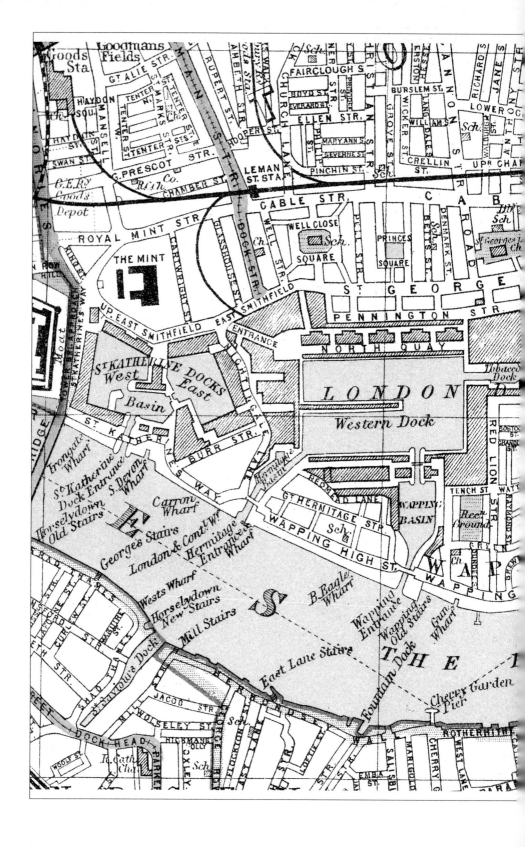

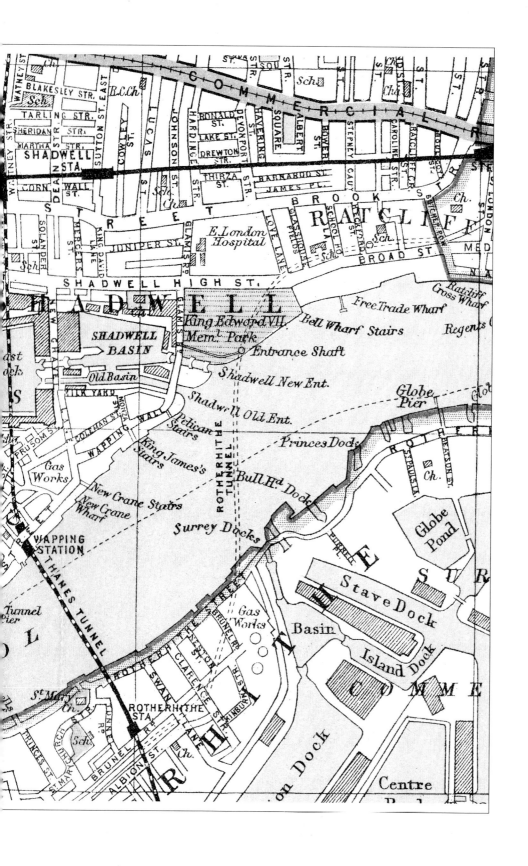

Bibliography and Sources

Books and Smaller Publications

The Battle of Cable Street 1936 (The Cable Street Group)

The Hermitage Shelter Minutes: December 1940 (History of Wapping Trust, 1990)

The Journal of the Oral History Society

Everybody's Family Doctor (Odhams Press, c. 1935)

Cornwell, Jocelyn, *Hard-Earned Lives: Accounts of Health and Illness from East London* (Tavistock, London, 1984)

Darby, Madge, *Tender Grace* Volumes I-V (Connor and Butler and History of Wapping Trust, 2002)

Darby, Madge, *Waeppa's People* (Connor and Butler and History of Wapping Trust, 1988)

Daunton, Claire (ed.), *The London Hospital Illustrated* (Bath Press, 1990)

Elmers, Chris and Werner, Alex, *Dockland Life: a Pictorial History of London's Docks 1860-1970* (Mainstream Publishing/ Museum of London, 1991)

Fishman, William, *The Streets of East London* (Duckworth, 1979)

Foakes, Grace, *My Part of the River* (Futura, 1988)

Fraser, Derek, *The Evolution of the British Welfare State* (Palgrave Macmillan, 2003)

Girling, Brian, *East Enders' Postcards* (Tempus Publishing, 2002)

Girling, Brian, *East End Neighbourhoods* (Tempus Publishing, 2005)

Greenhalgh, Trisha and Hurwitz, Brian (ed.), *Narrative Based Medicine* (BMJ Books 1998)

Hanshaw, Patrick, *Nothing is Forever* (Wapping neighbourhood, 1992)

Hanshaw, Patrick, *All my Yesterdays* (Tower Hamlets Council, 1996)

Hopkinson, Tom (ed.), *Picture Post 1938-1950* (Chatto & Windus, 1984)

Kemp, Ellen, 'Don't Let Them See You Cry' (Extracts from unpublished memoir) *Rising East* Vol. 2 No. 3 (Cambridge University Press)

Lewey, Frank, *Cockney Campaign* (Stanley Paul, 1944, reissued by Tower Hamlets Local History Library, 1999)

Menzies, Lucy, *Father Wainwright* (Longmans, 1947)

O'Neill, Gilda, *Pull No More Bines* (The Women's Press, 1990)

O'Neill, Gilda, *My East End* (Penguin, 2000)

Palmer, Alan, *The East End* (John Murray, 1989)

Perks, Robert and Thomson, Alistair, *The Oral History Reader* (Routledge, 2000)

Porter, Roy, *The Greatest Benefit to Mankind* (Harper Collins, 1997)

Rosten, Leo, *The Joys of Yiddish* (Penguin, 1971)

Schweitzer, Pam (ed.) *Can we Afford the Doctor?* (Age Exchange, 1985)

Schweitzer, Pam (ed.) *Memories of a Working River* (Age Exchange, 1989)

Spring Rice, Margery, *Working Class Wives* (Pelican, 1939)

Stevenson, John, *Social Conditions in Britain Between the Wars* (Penguin, 1977)

Taylor, Rosemary and Lloyd, Christopher, *Stepney, Bethnal Green and Poplar in Old Photographs* (Sutton Publishing, 1995)

Taylor, Rosemary and Lloyd, Christopher, *The Changing East End* (Sutton Publishing, 1997)

Taylor, Rosemary and Lloyd, Christopher, *The East End at Work* (Sutton Publishing, 1999)

Taylor, Rosemary, *Hannah Billig*

Thompson, Paul, *The Voice of the Past* (Oxford University Press, 2000)

Various, *Dr Jelley, The Threepenny Doctor of Hackney* (Centerprise Trust, 1983)
Wear, Andrew (ed.), *Medicine in Society* (Cambridge University Press, 1992)
Worley, Vincent, *The Story of Catholic Wapping* (1971)
Worth, Jennifer, *Call the Midwife* (Merton Books, 2002)
Worth, Jennifer, *Shadows of the Workhouse* (Merton Books, 2005)
Young, Michael and Wilmott, Peter, *Family and Kinship in East London* (Pelican, 1980)

Libraries and Archives

Museum in Docklands
Tower Hamlets Local History Library
Royal College of General Practitioners
The Women's Library
British Library National Sound Archive
St Peter's Church Archives
St Patrick's Church Archive
London Metropolitan Archive
Wapping River Police Museum
Wellcome Library

Other local titles published by The History Press

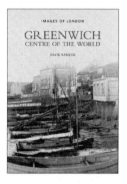

London A Century in the City
BRIAN GIRLING

This fascinating collection of images explores the changes taking place in the London from 1850-1950. From shoe-black scenes to war ruins, the selection shows a surprisingly varied range of activities and views. *London: A Century in the City* is a valuable pictorial history which will reawaken nostalgic memories for some, whilst offering a unique glimpse into the past for it others.

978 07524 4507 6

Greenwich Centre of the World
DAVID RAMZAN

Greenwich has always been well-known for its position on the meridian line, however as David Ramzan illustrates in this new book, the area has a rich history with its commercial and industrial businesses in the town or on the river, and its naval and military connections. Illustrated with over 200 images, the book brings to life bygone days when Greenwich was a major tourist attraction. Although today much of Greenwich's heritage has been lost, this book will show what a wonderful place it was and still is today.

978 07524 4260 0

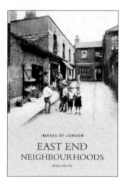

Croydon and Waddon
RAYMOND WHEELER

This fascinating new book illustrates central Croydon and its adjoining district, Waddon, from the nineteenth century onwards. Arranged thematically, the compilation contains over 200 photographs, many selected from private collections. In particular, changing types of transport, fashion, shops, work, recreation and the way of life of a busy town are covered in this portrait of how Croydonians used to live.

978 07524 4301 0

East End Neighbourhoods
BRIAN GIRLING

The River Thames, with its docks, wharves and associated industries, has been a source of livelihood for generations of East Enders living in the historic riverside neighbourhoods of the former Metropolitan Boroughs of Stepney, Poplar and adjacent areas. From images of the maritime stores of old nautical Limehouse and the silk-weaving houses in Bethnal Green at the turn of the twentieth century, to views of the prefabs in Poplar after the Second World War, this selection recalls how life was lived in the tightly packed streets of the East End.

978 07524 3519 0

If you are interested in purchasing other books published by The History Press, or in case you have difficulty finding any History Press books in your local bookshop, you can also place orders directly through our website

www.thehistorypress.co.uk